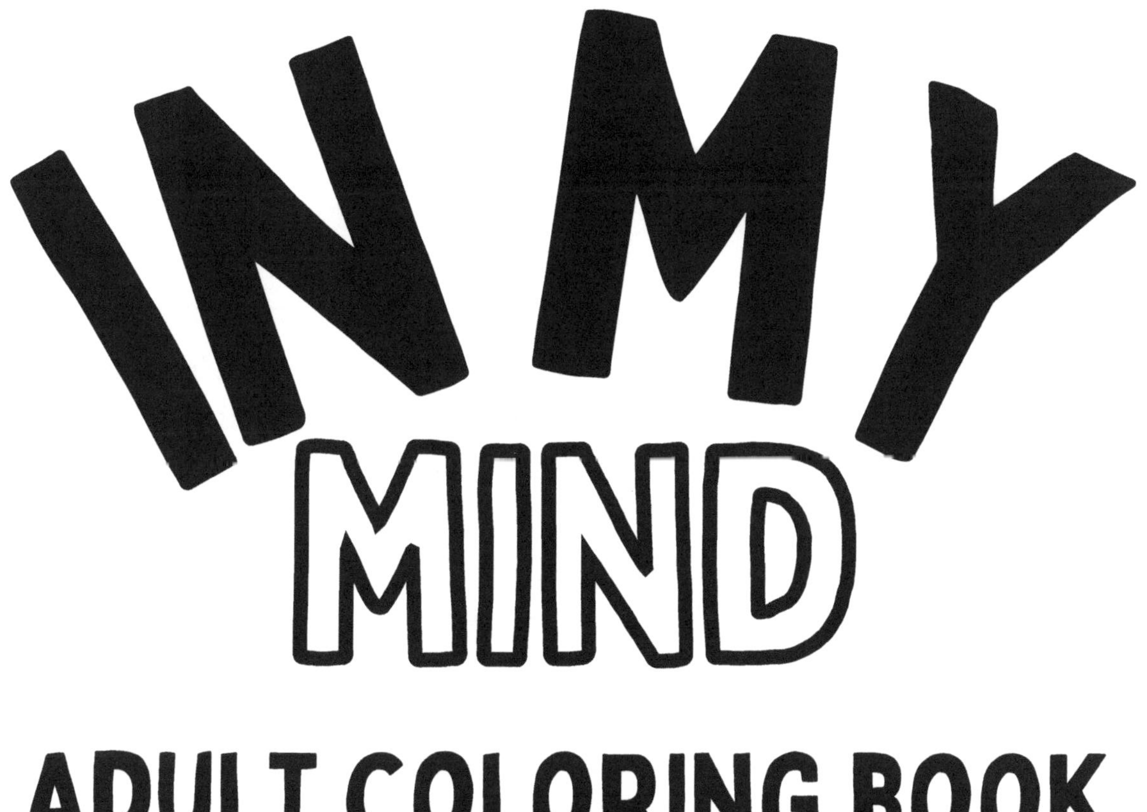

ADULT COLORING BOOK

ARTIST BYRON L. EDWARDS

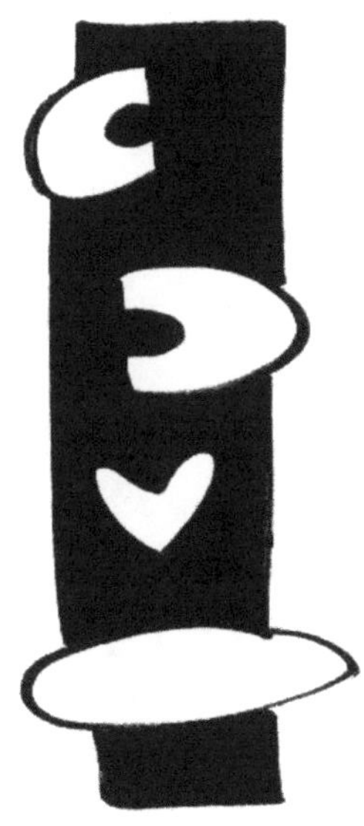

MYND MATTERS PUBLISHING
715 PEACHTREE STREET NE
SUITES 100 & 200
ATLANTA, GA 30308
WWW.MYNDMATTERSPUBLISHING.COM

ISBN: 978-1-957092-53-9 (PBK)

FIRST EDITION

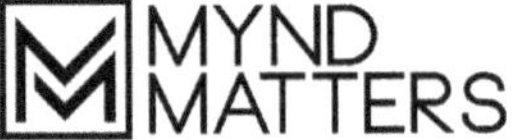

Exploring Your Emotions

Can you name your emotions?

How would you descibe the below faces?

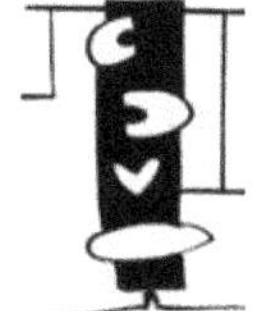 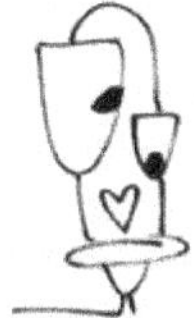 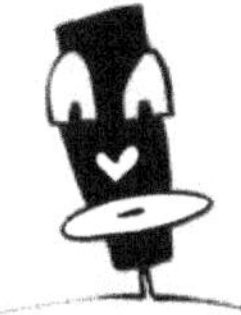 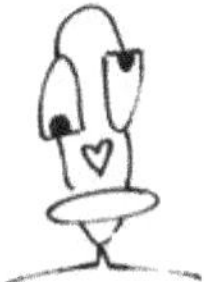 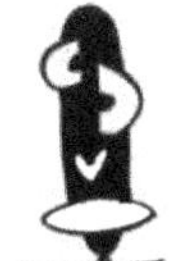

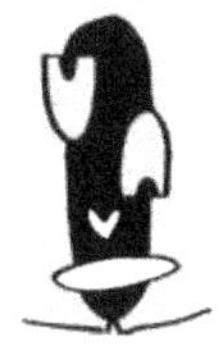 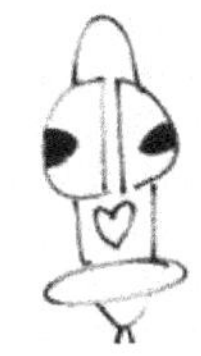 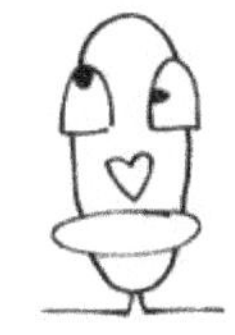 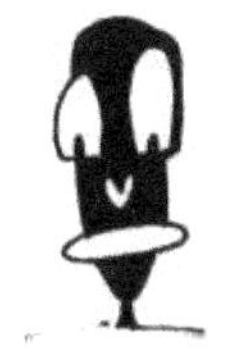 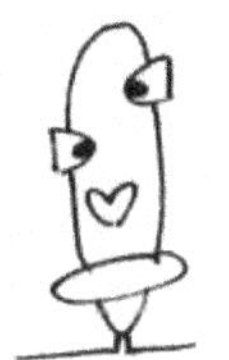

SILLY	CONCERNED	SHOCKED
FUN	ANNOYED	UNWELL
SATISFIED	AMAZED	HORRIFIED
UNSURE	SURPRISED	HAPPY
SAD	UPSET	JOYFUL
DISTRESSED	DISMAYED	PLEASED
EXCITED	THRILLED	IRRITATED
MAD	ANGRY	ANXIOUS

Exploring Your Emotions

Can you recognize your emotions?

Read and answer using ONE word.

How do you feel when you wake up? _______________________________

How do you feel when you fail? _______________________________

How do you feel when things don't go your way? _______________________________

How do you feel when someone hurts you? _______________________________

How do you feel before going to sleep? _______________________________

Can you express and explain your emotions?

Think how you feel at this moment and draw it. Then explain why you feel this way.

THE FEELINGS OF MY MIND

CONCERNED	SILLY	SHOCKED
ANNOYED	FUN	UNWELL
SURPRISED	UNSURE	HAPPY
UPSET	SAD	JOYFUL
AMAZED	SATISFIED	HORRIFIED
DISMAYED	DISTRESSED	PLEASED
THRILLED	EXCITED	IRRITATED
ANGRY	MAD	ANXIOUS

Ww

W is for well.

COLOR THEORY

color theory is the body of practical guidance for color
mixing and the visual effects of a specific color combination

This is a color

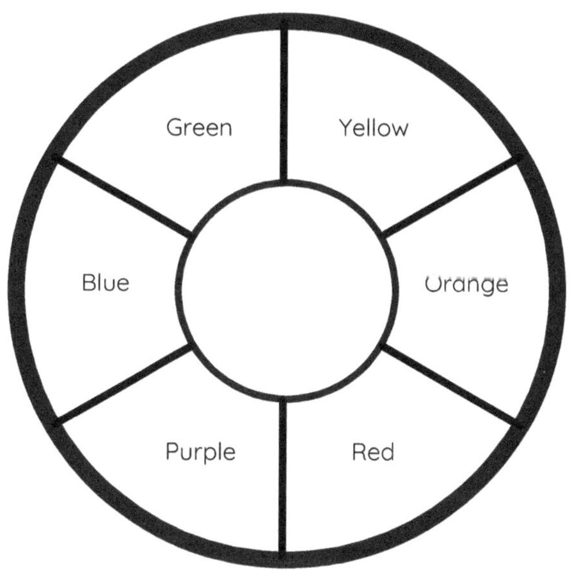

This is what happens

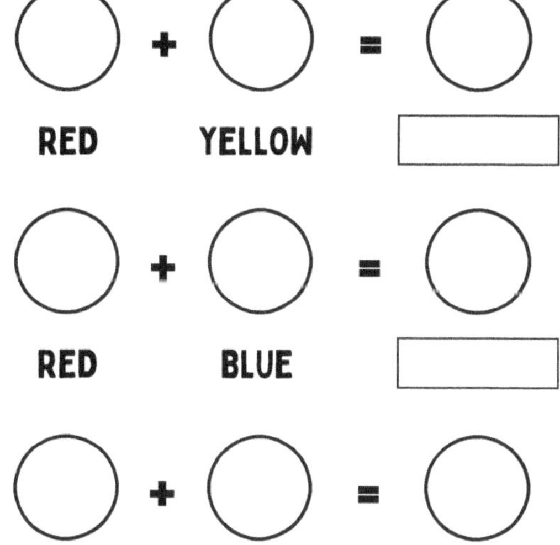

Some color schemes are:

PRIMARY COLORS

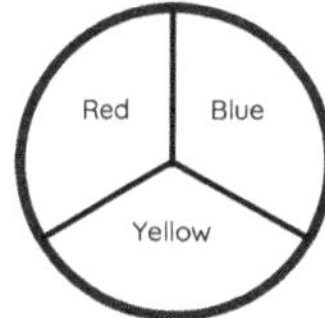

THEY MAKE THE OTHER COLORS.

SECONDARY COLORS

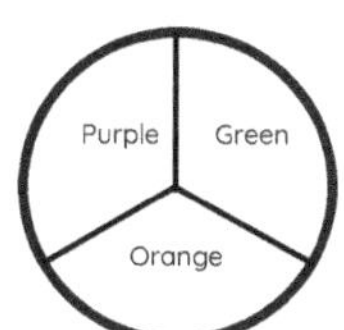

THEY ARE MADE BY MIXING PRIMARY COLORS.

WARM COLORS

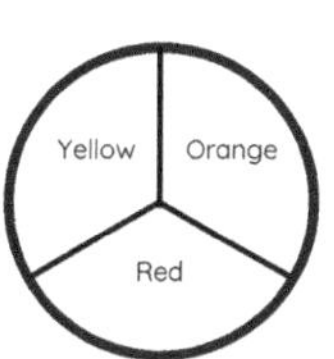

THEY MAKE YOU THINK OF WARM THINGS.

COOL COLORS

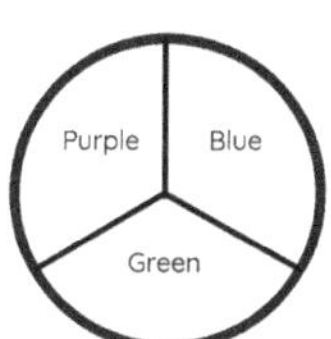

THEY MAKE YOU THINK OF COOL THINGS.

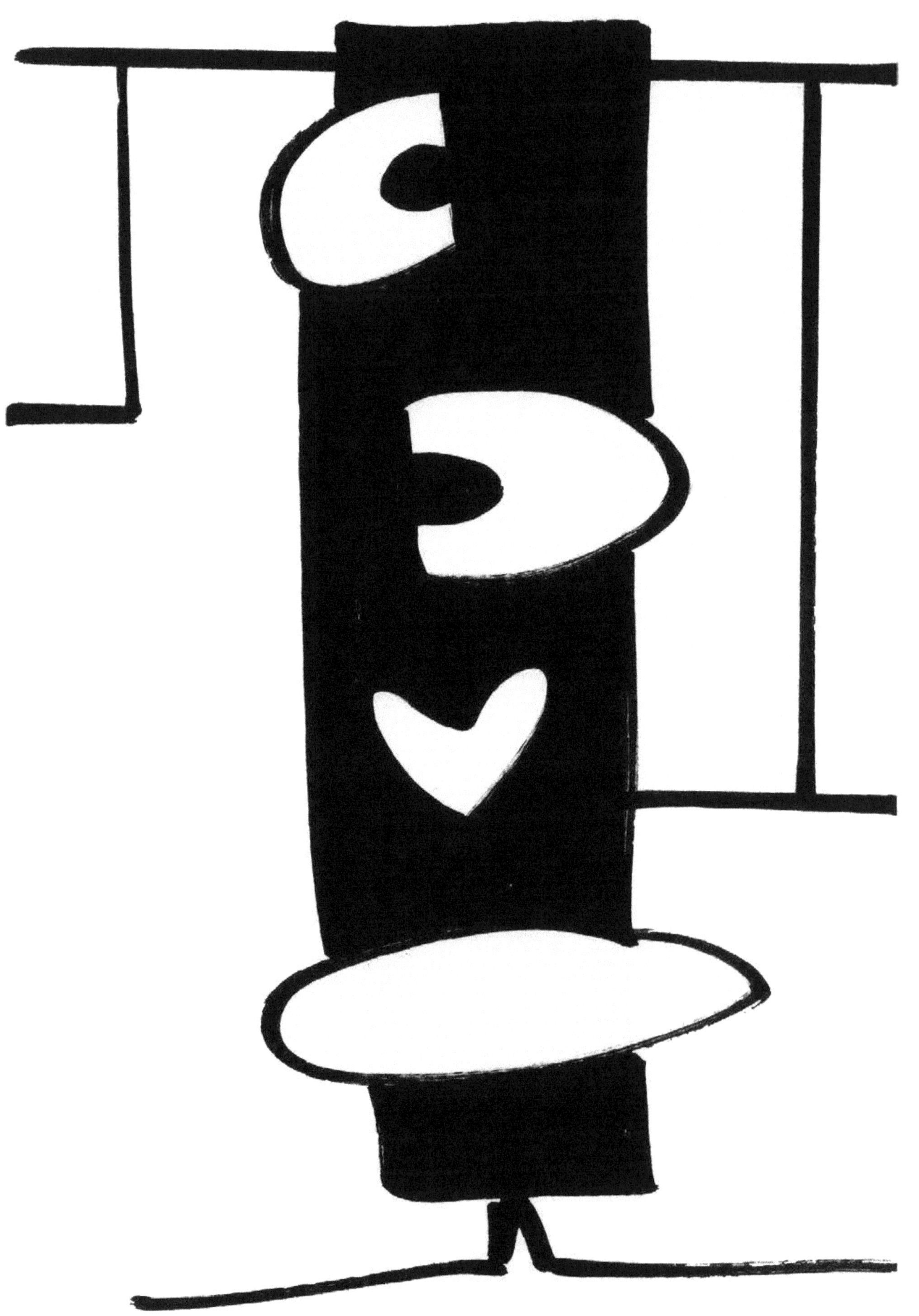

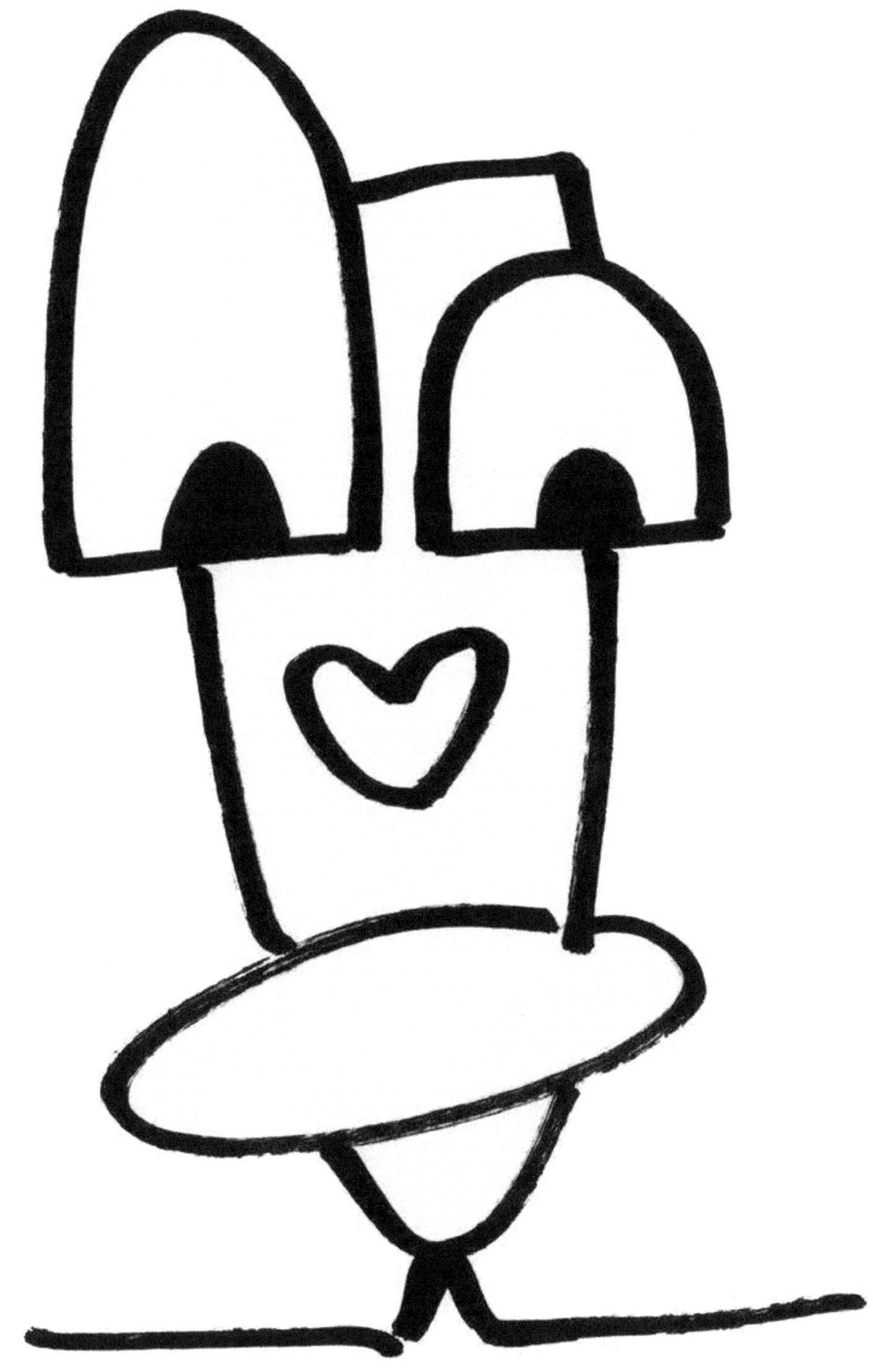

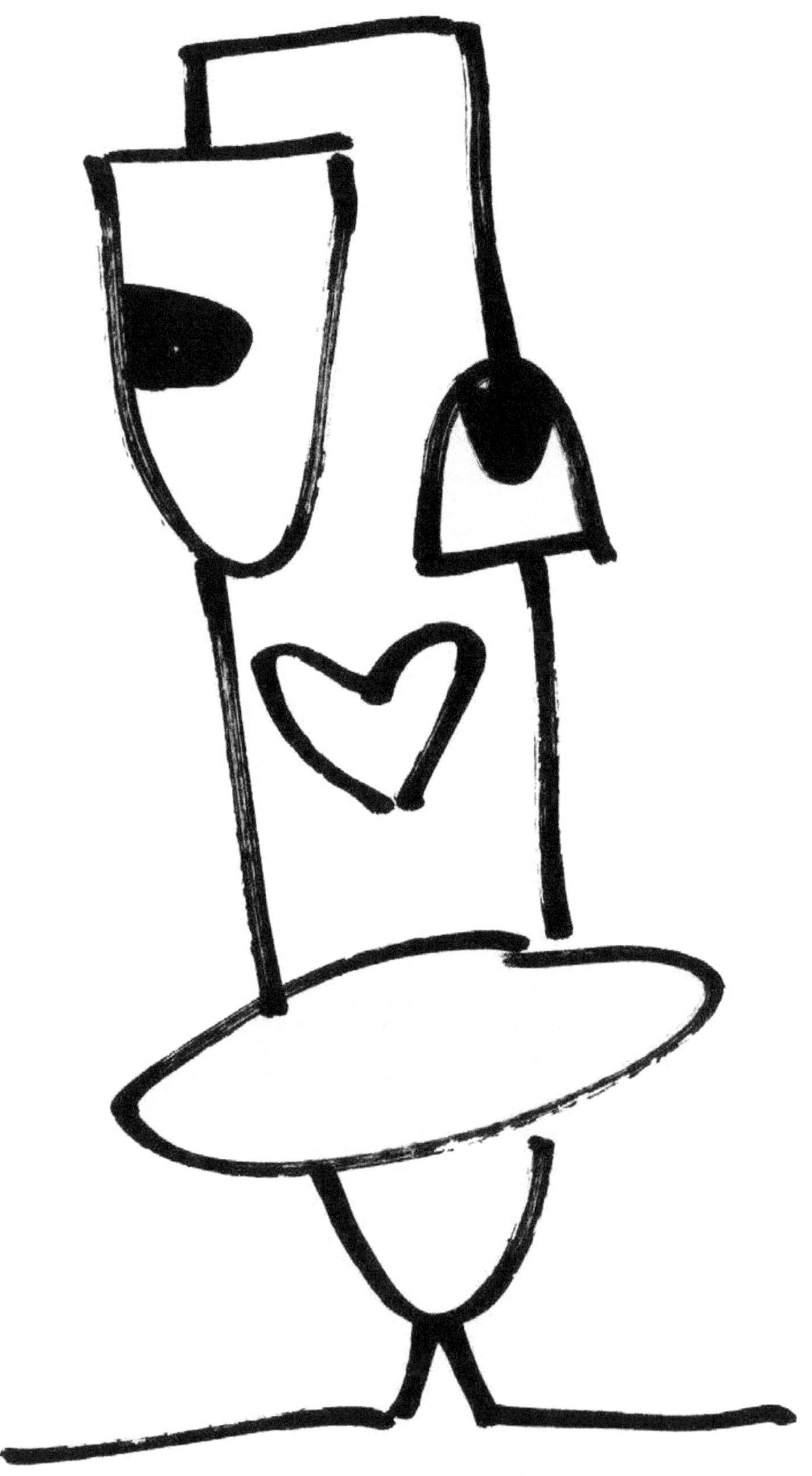

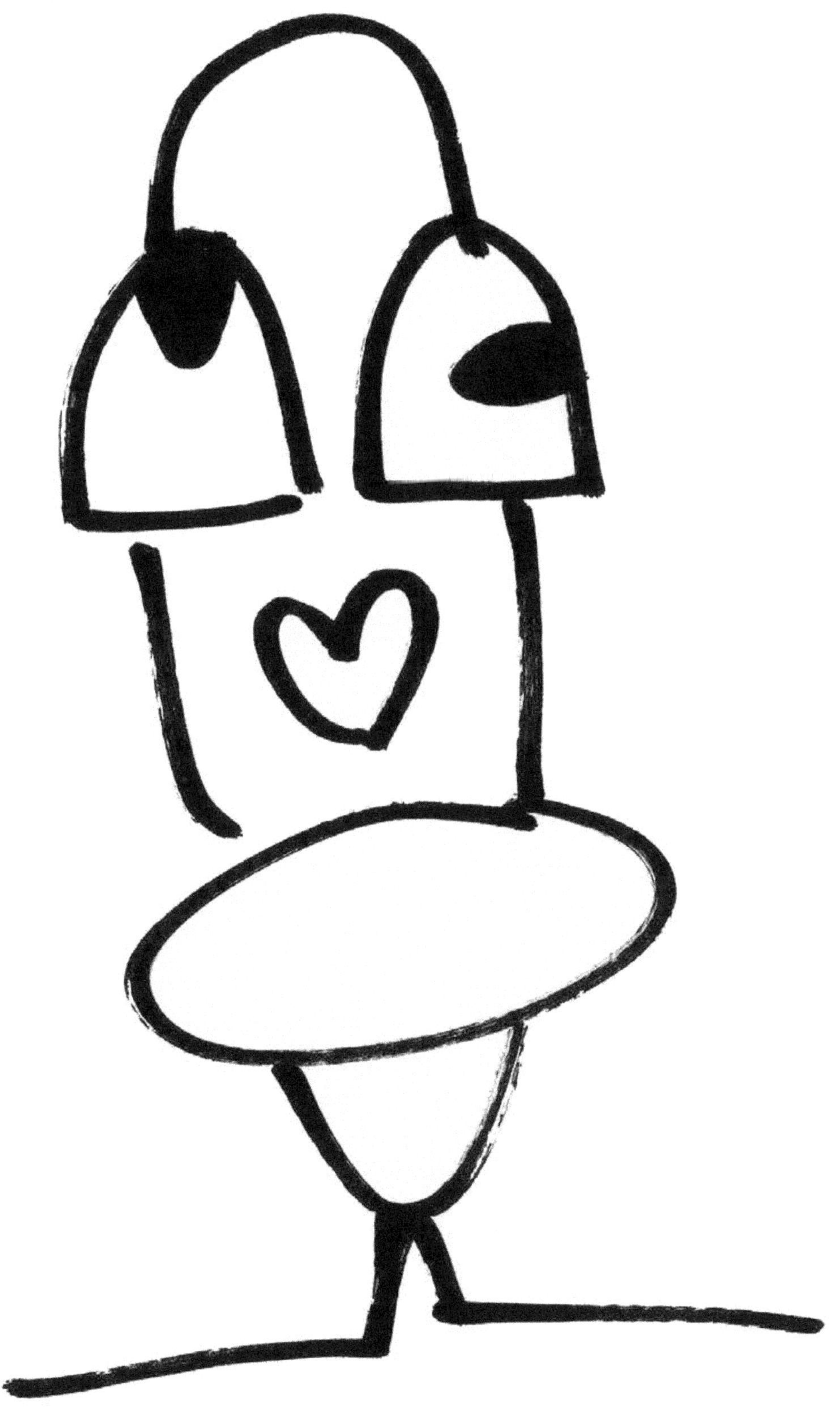

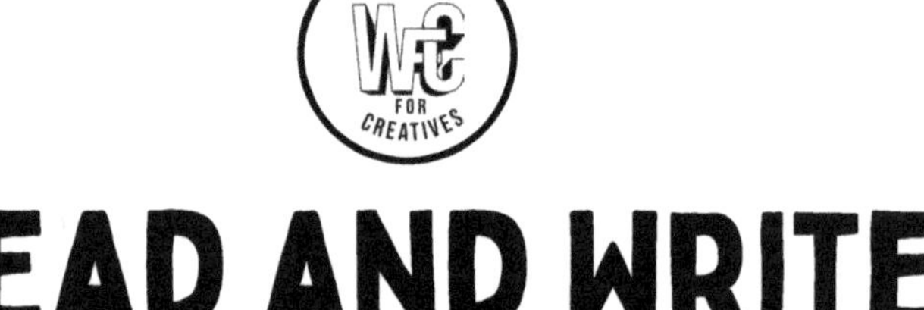

READ AND WRITE

Read the sentences and complete the answer.

Read	Write
I hate/love my job; I want to...	
I need a vacation; I want to go to...	
Life is good! I'm glad I have...	
I love... This feels great!	

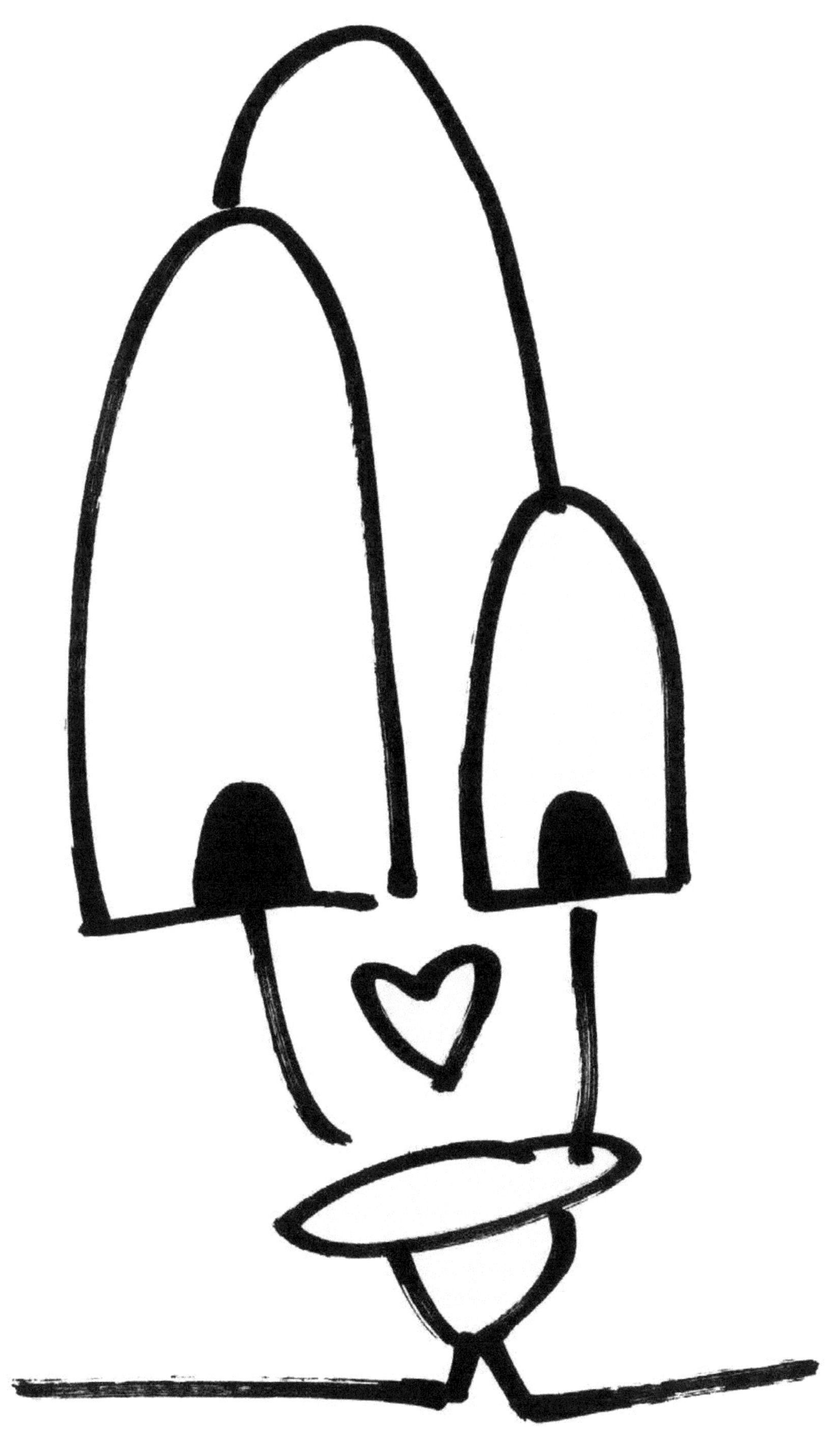

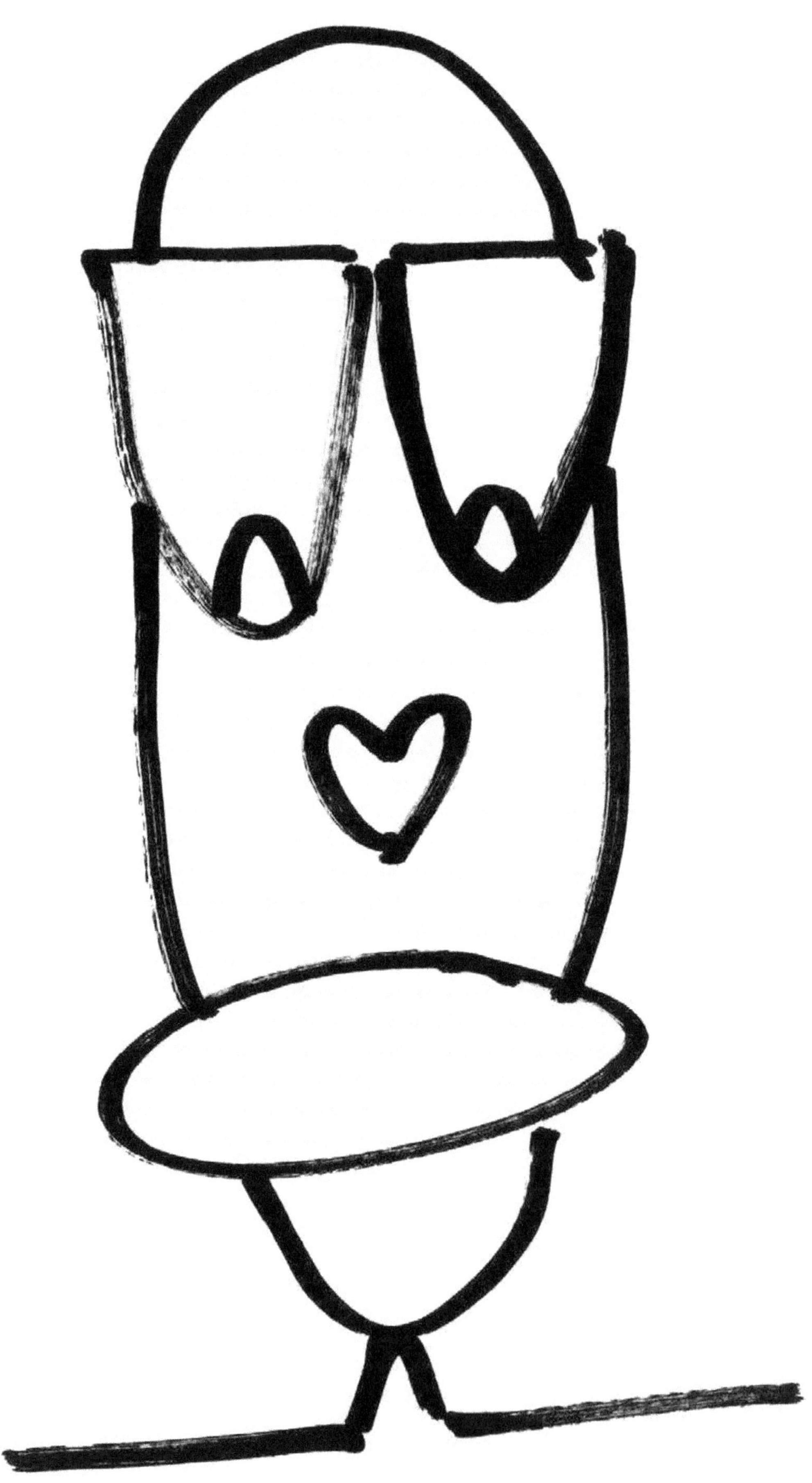

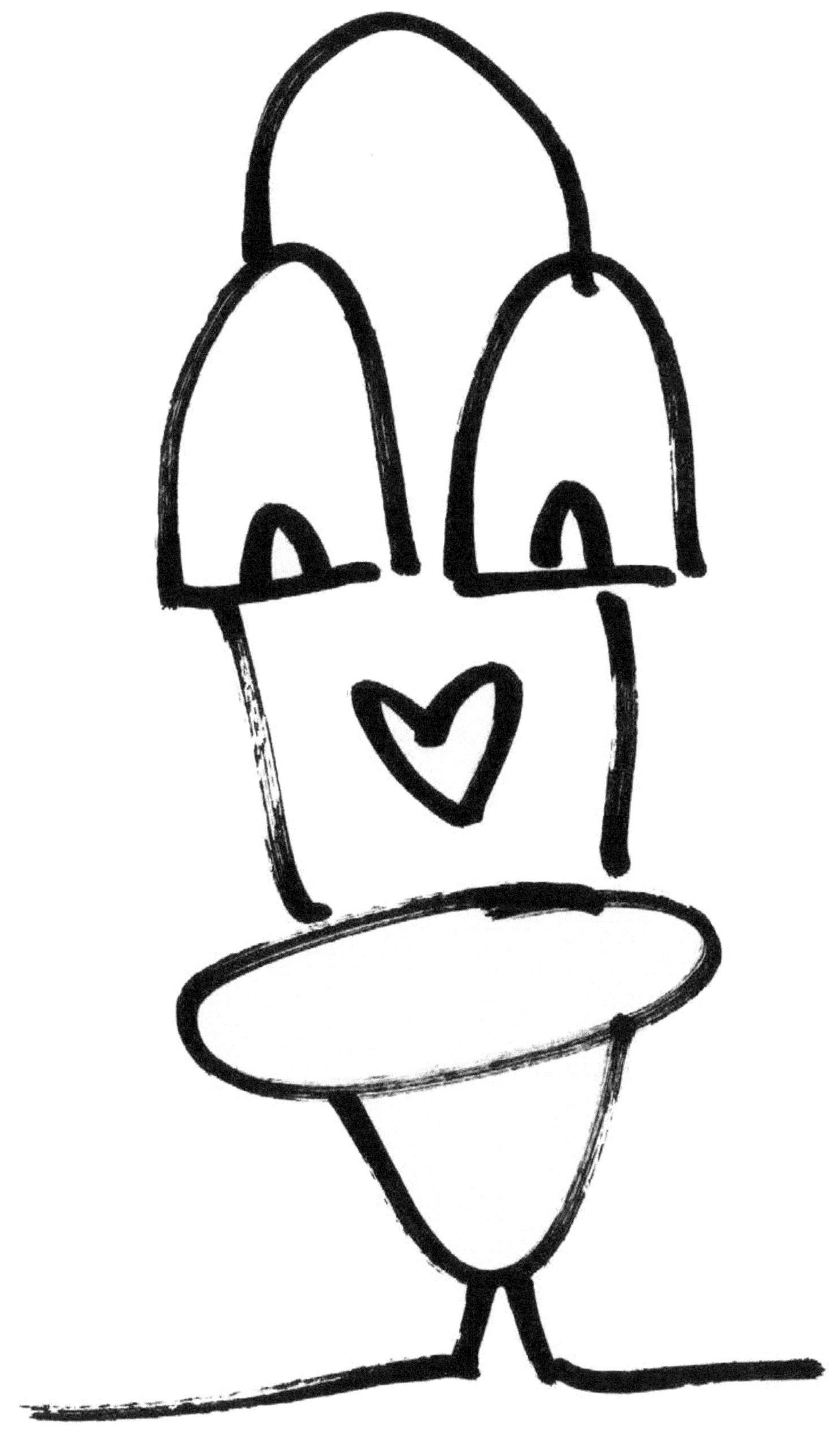

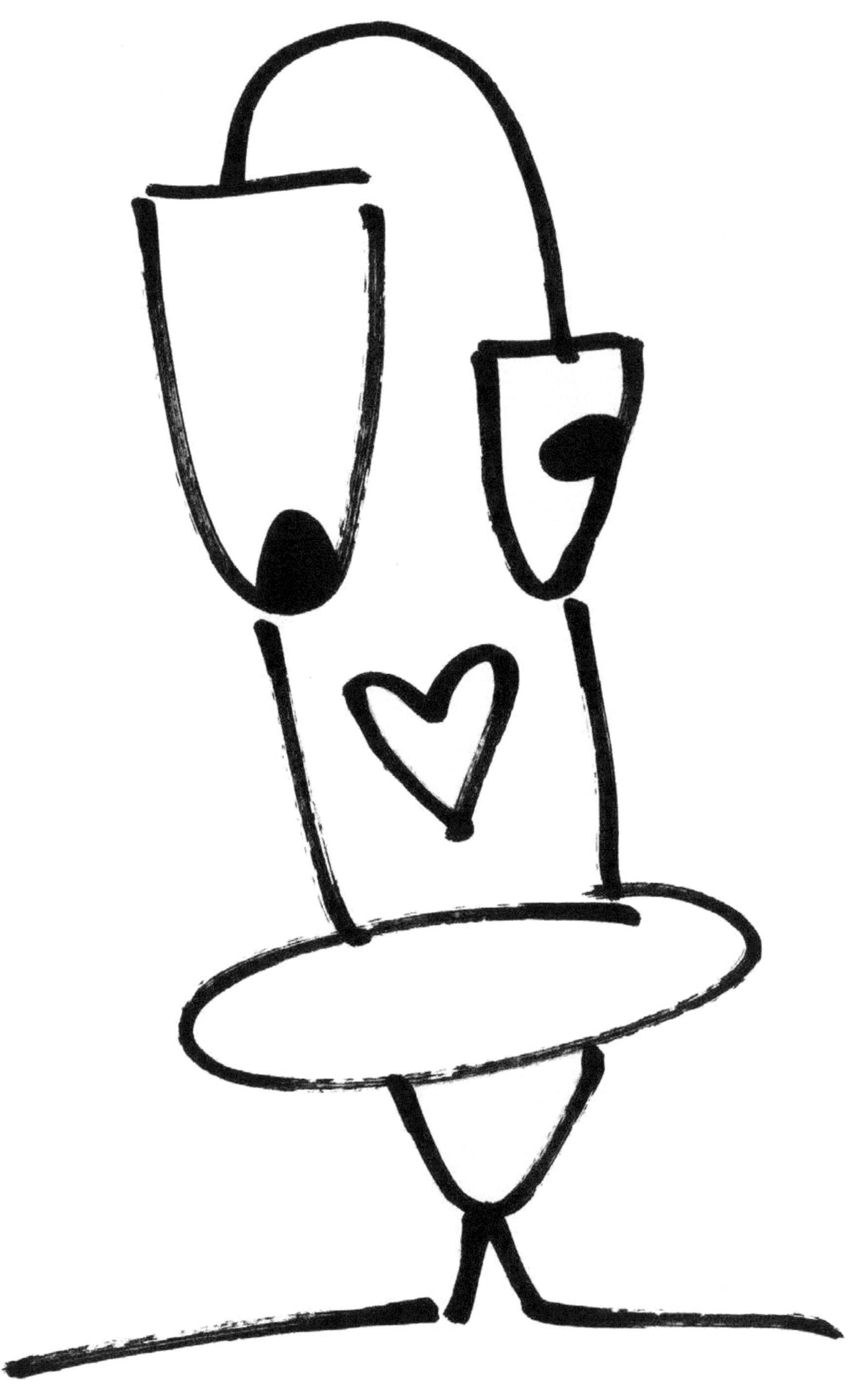

WHO - WHAT - WHERE
WHEN - WHY - HOW

WRITE YOUR STORY!

WHO Who is it about?	**WHAT** What happened?	**WHERE** Where did it take place?

WHEN When did it take place?	**WHY** Why did it happen?	**HOW** How did it happen?

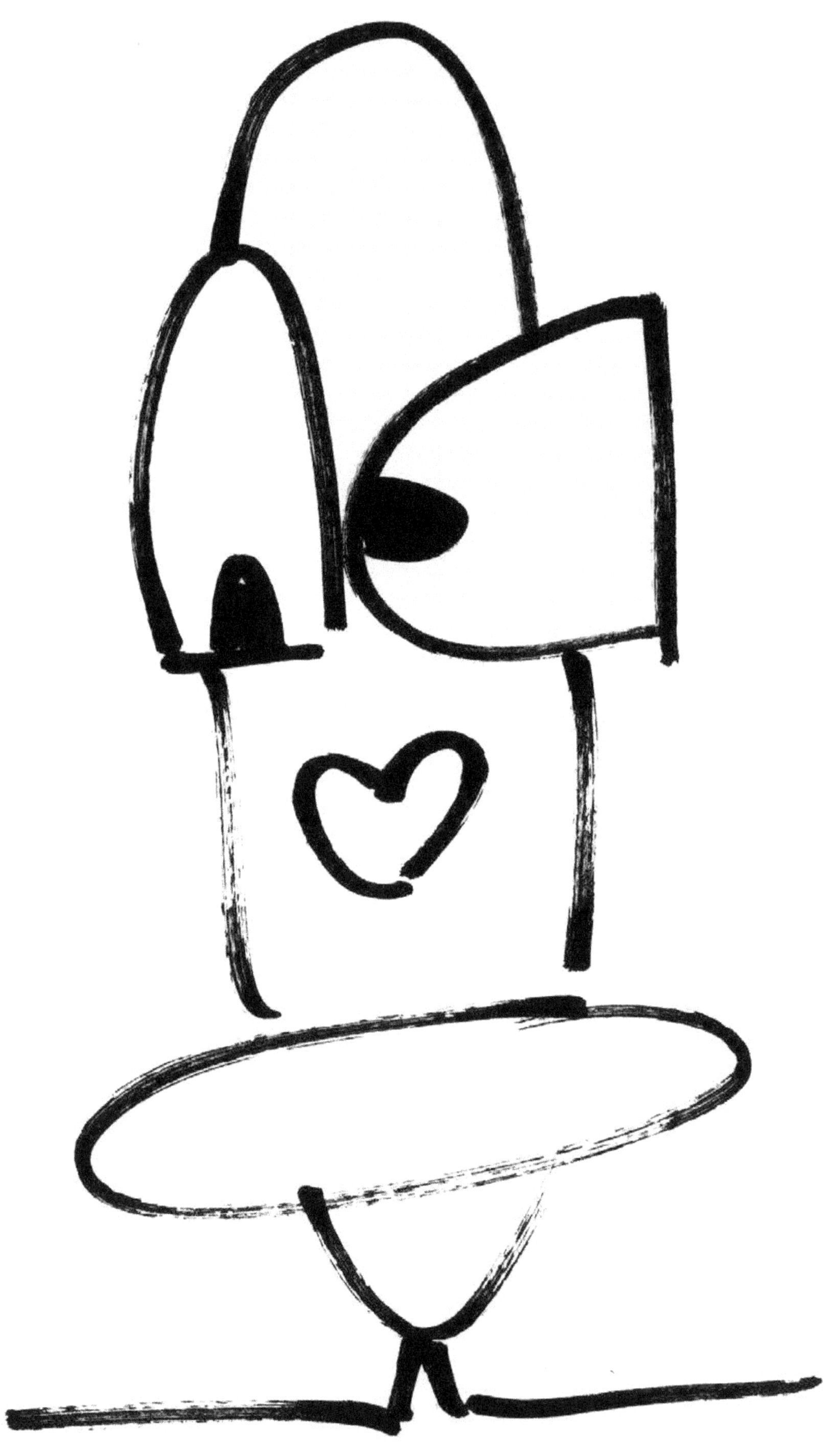

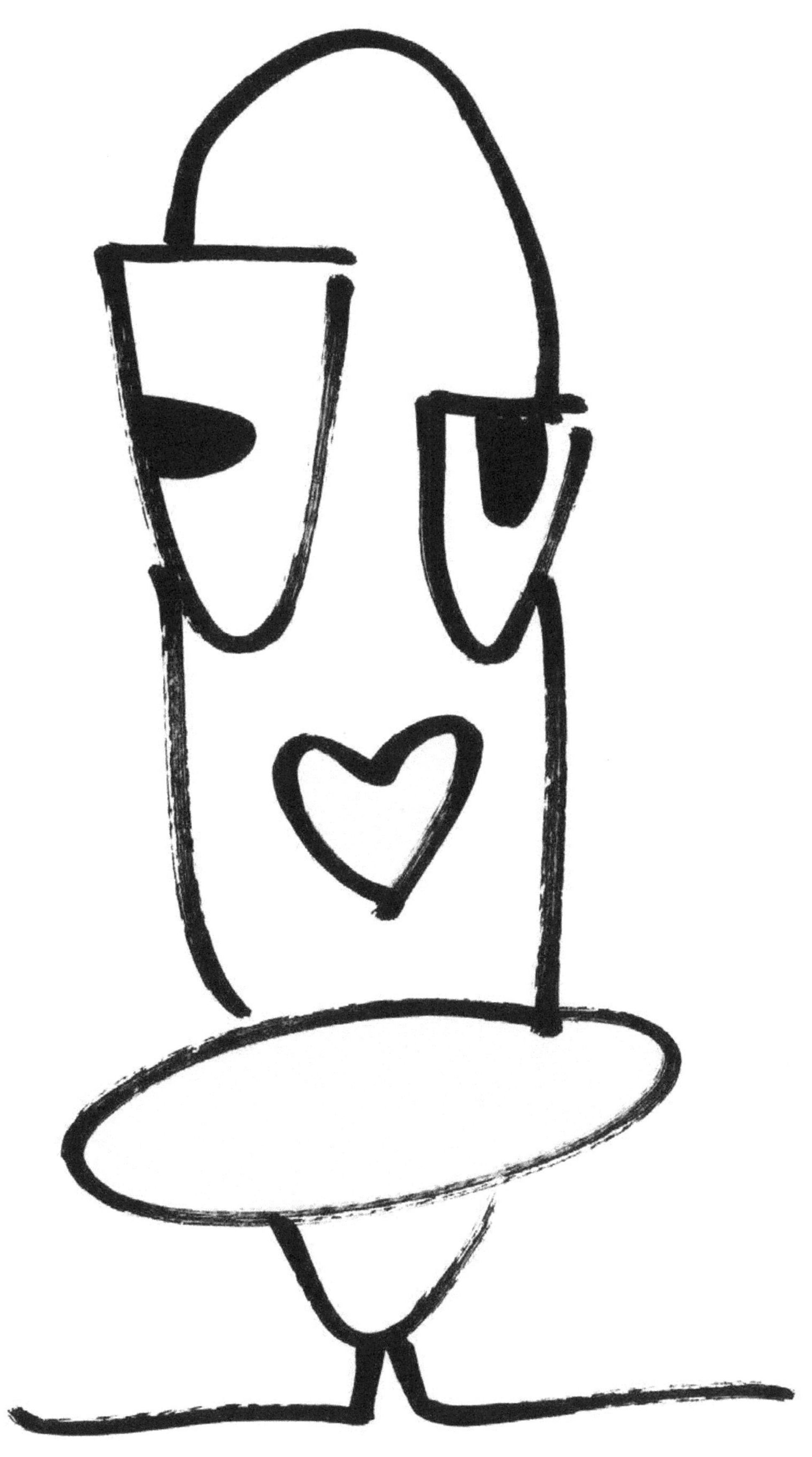

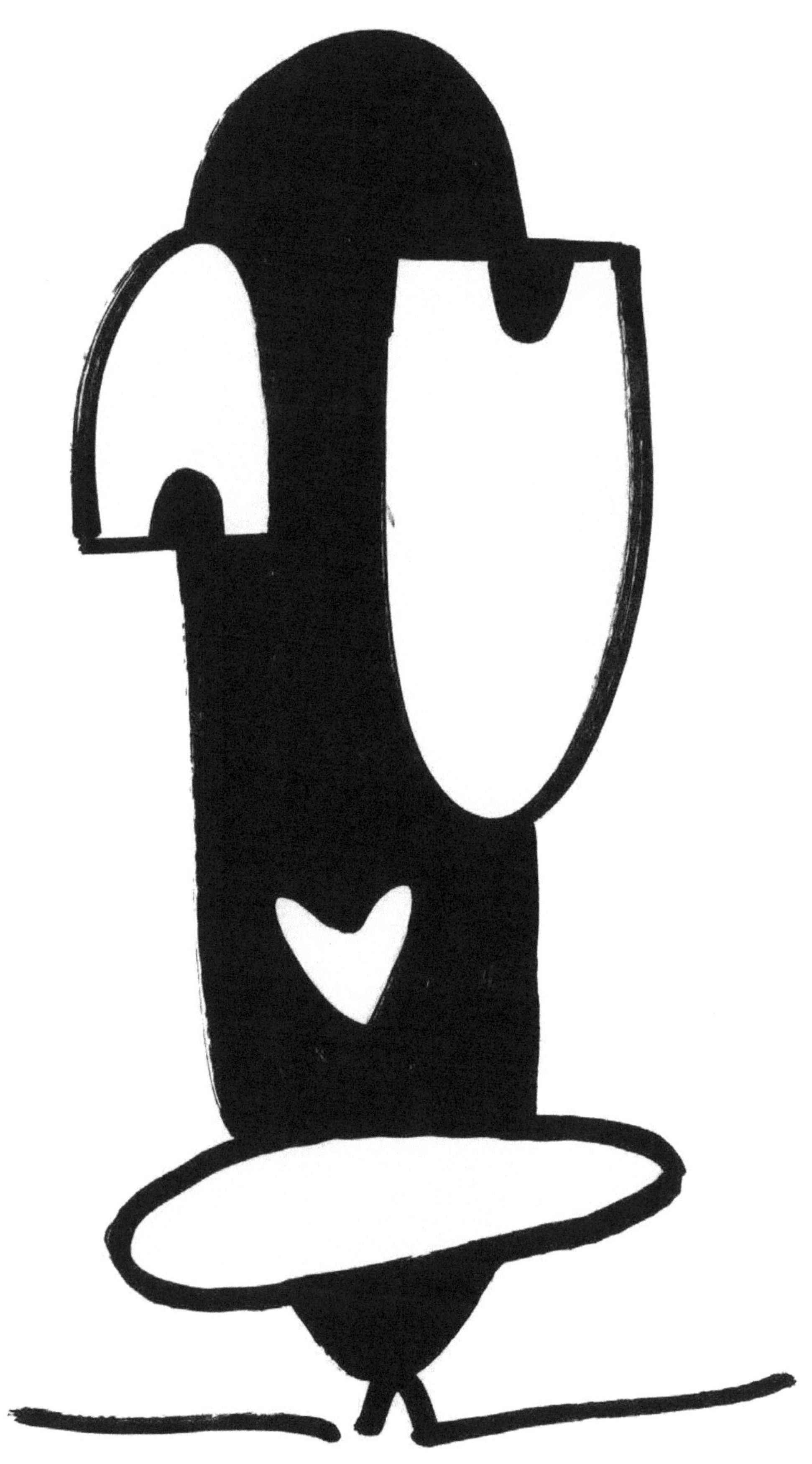

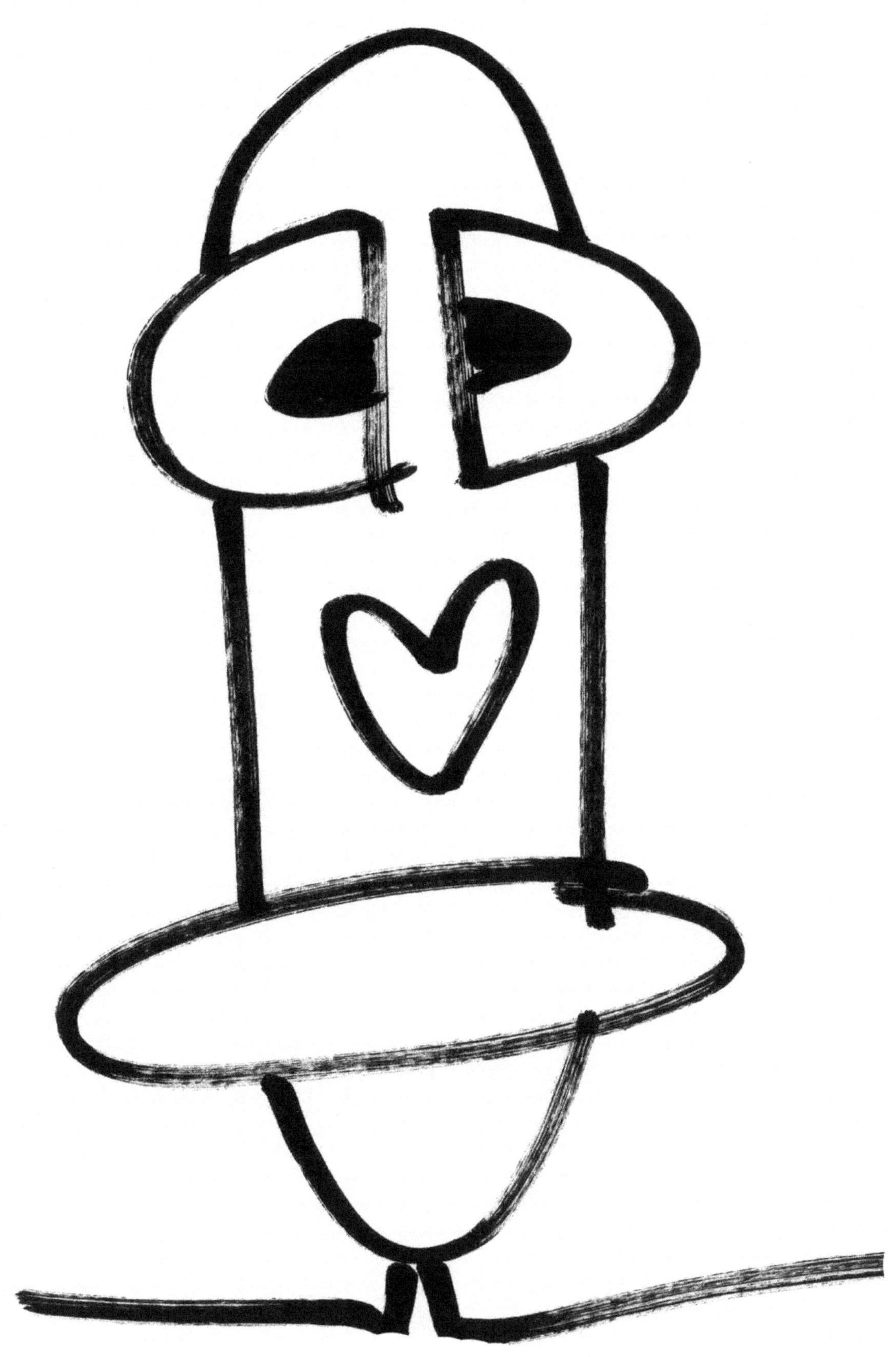

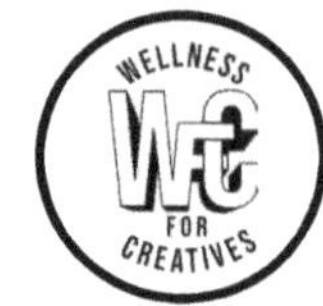

DATE: _______________

CHECK-IN

I am feeling: _______________________

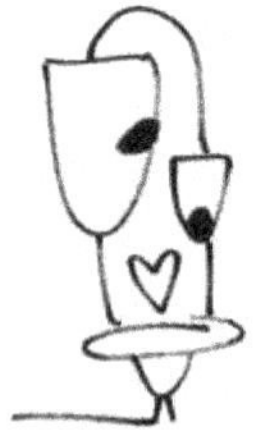 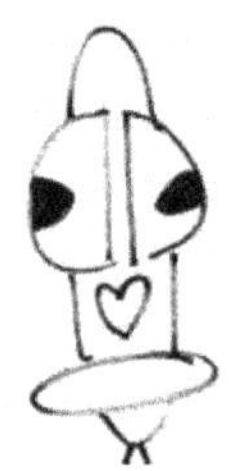 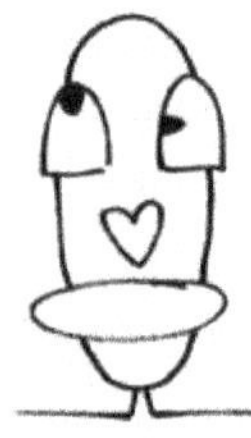 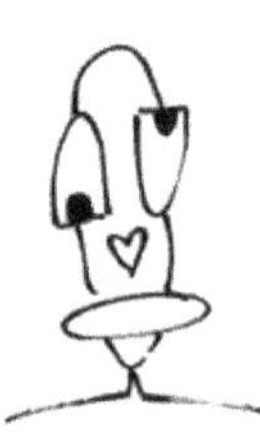 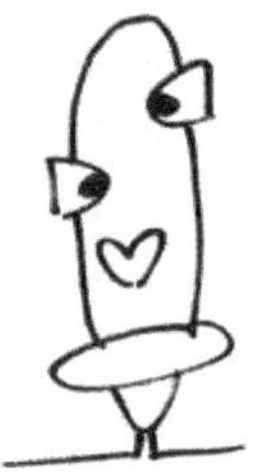

Something I want to change:

____

____

Something I want to learn:

____

____

Something I want to grow:

____

____

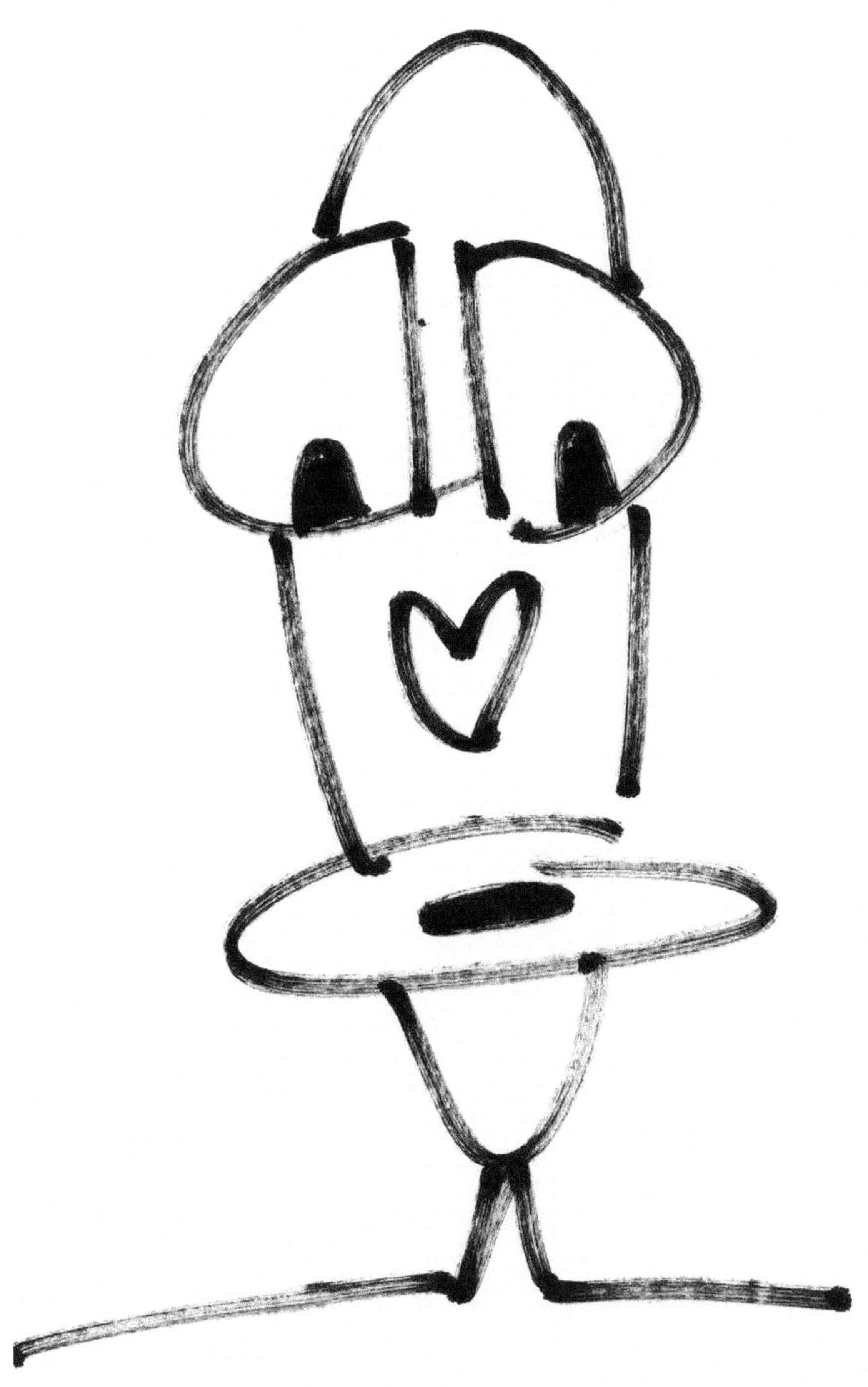

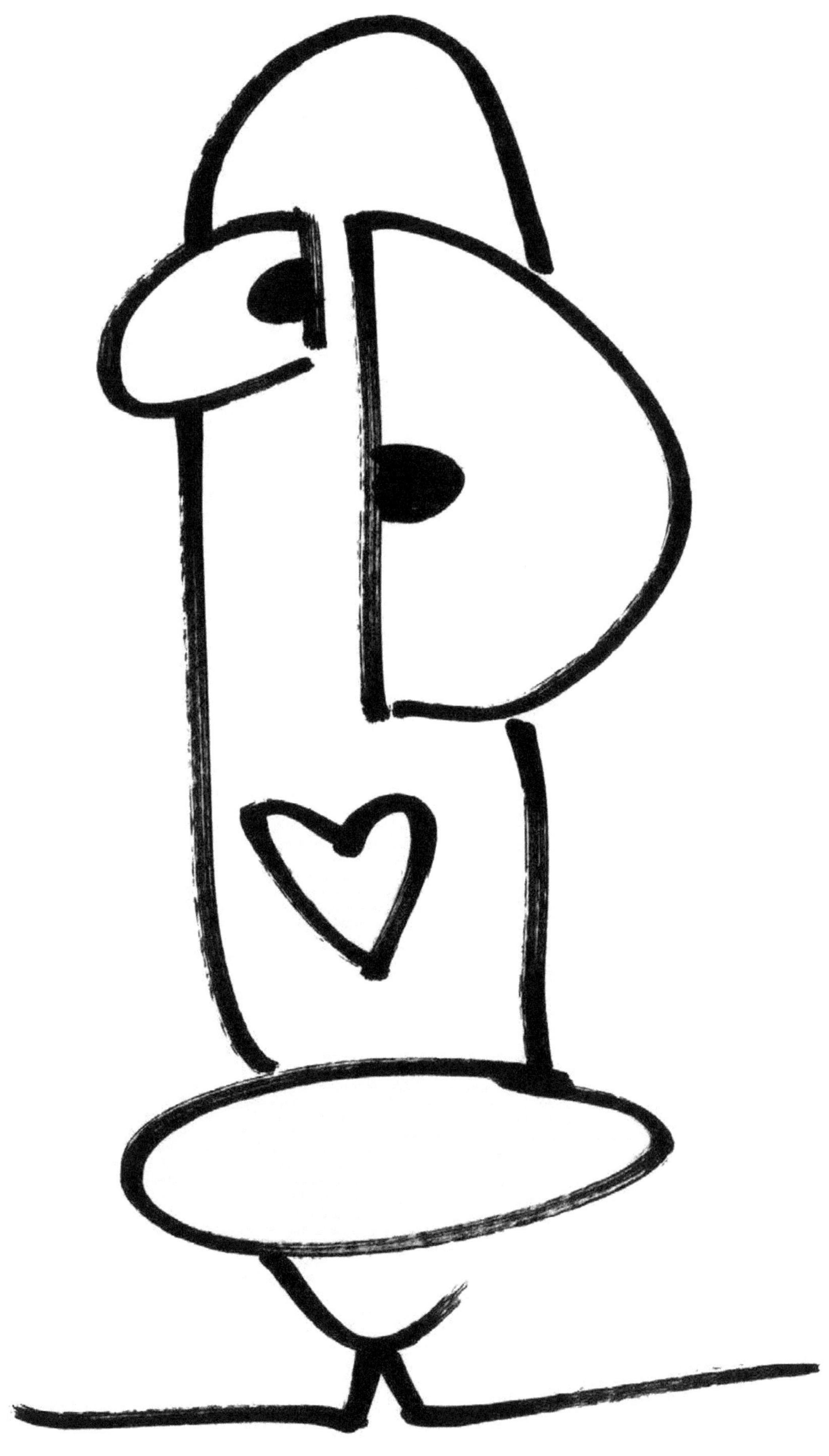

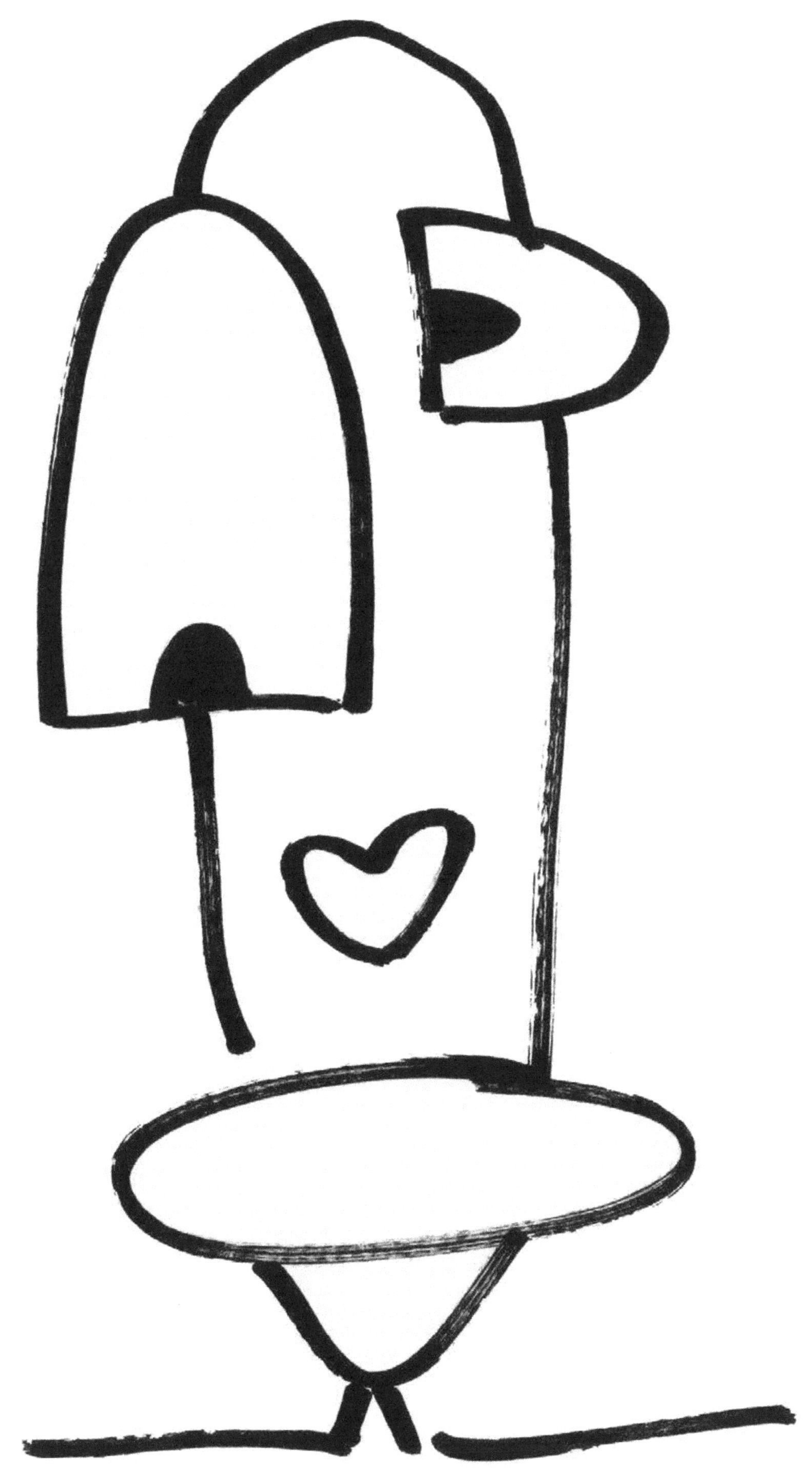

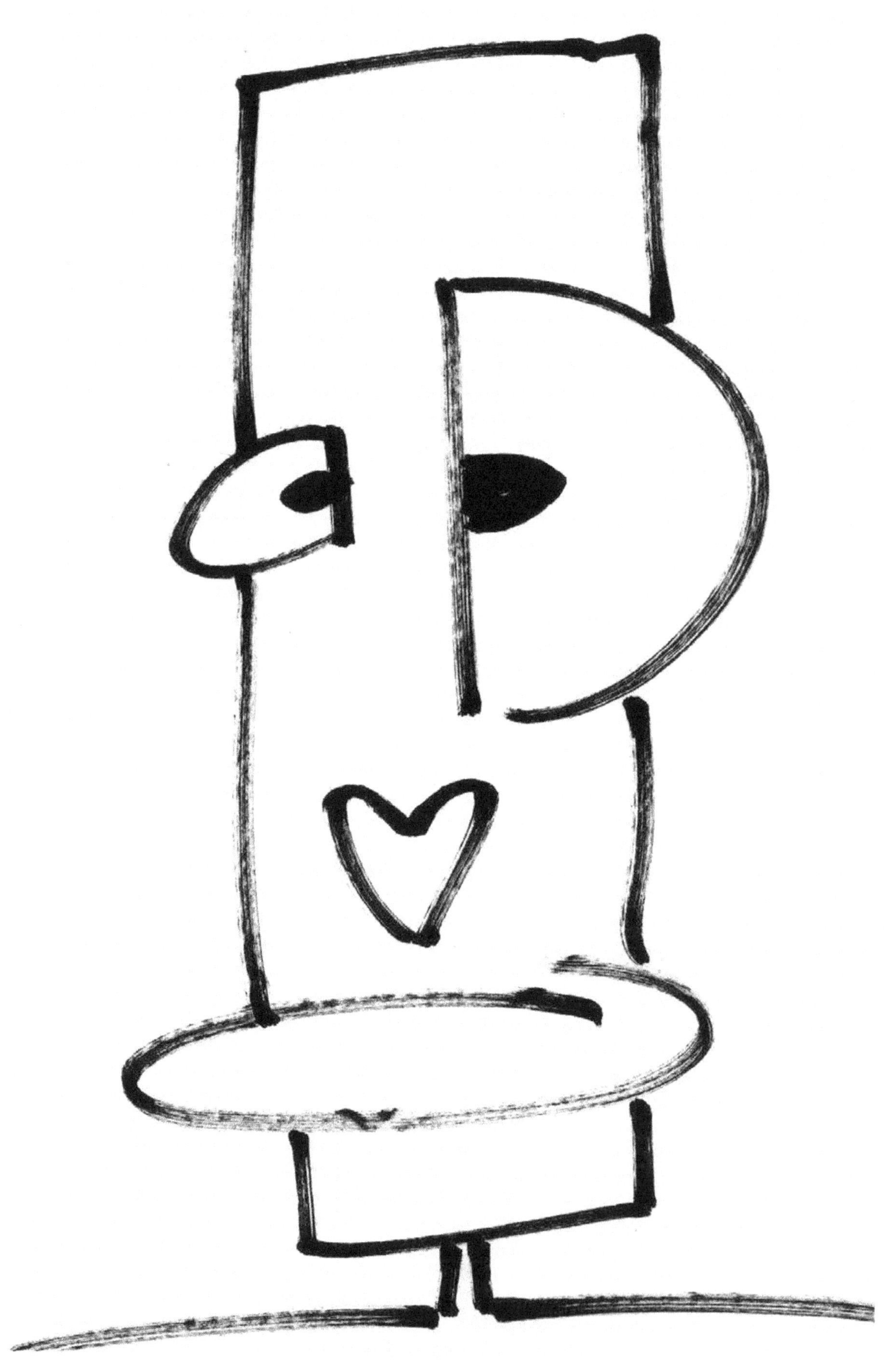

ONE THING I DO REALLY WELL

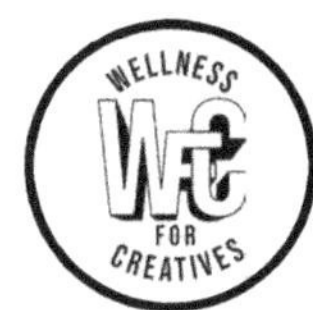

POSITIVE SELF SPEAK

Positive self-talk is an internal narrative you create for and about yourself.
Positive self-talk can have a positive effect on how we see ourselves, which
can positively affect the world around us.

COMPLETE THE STORY USING THE WRITING PROMPT BELOW.

ONE THING I DO REALLY WELL IS ____

____

____

____

____

____

____

____

____

____

____

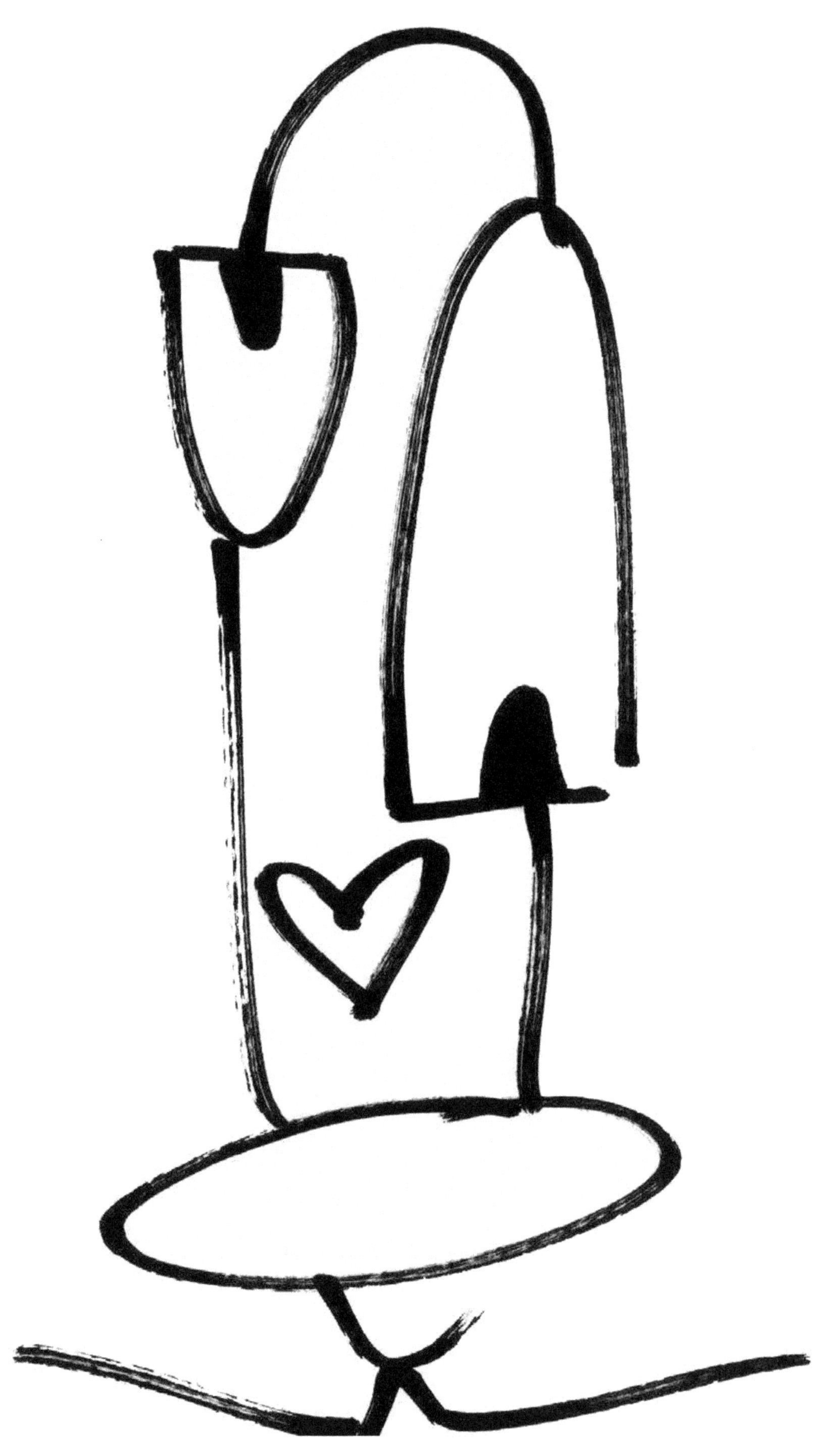

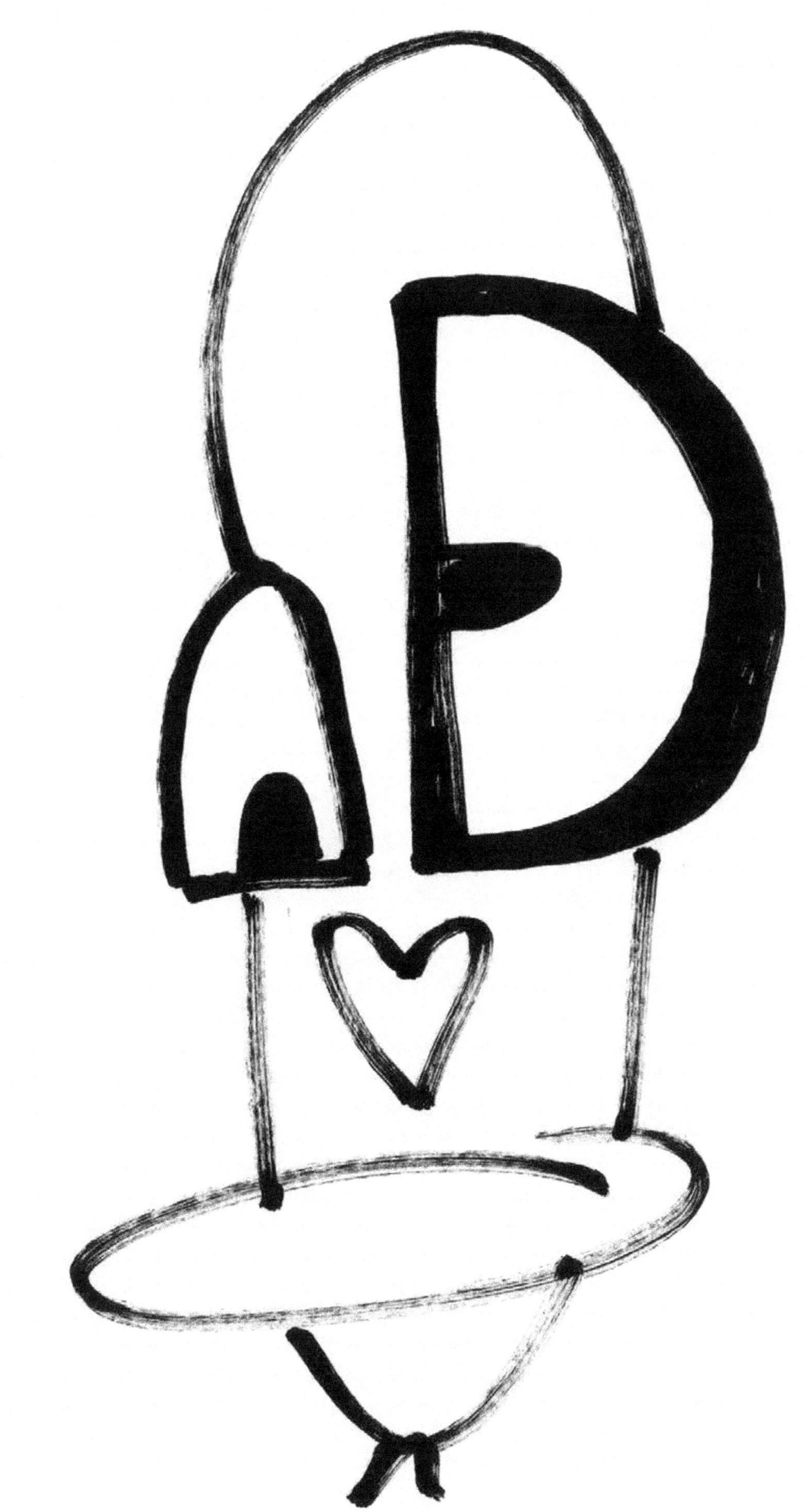

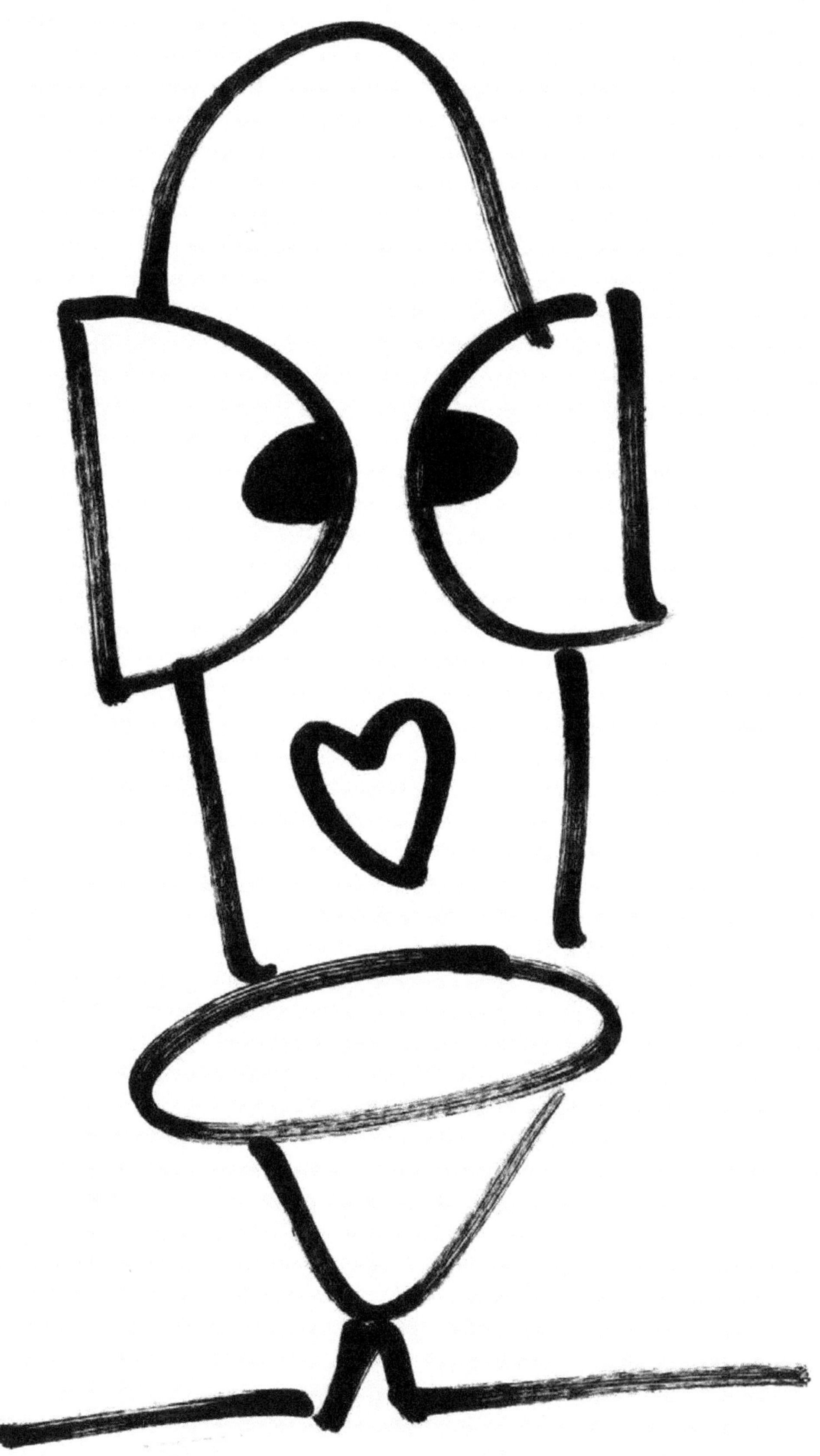

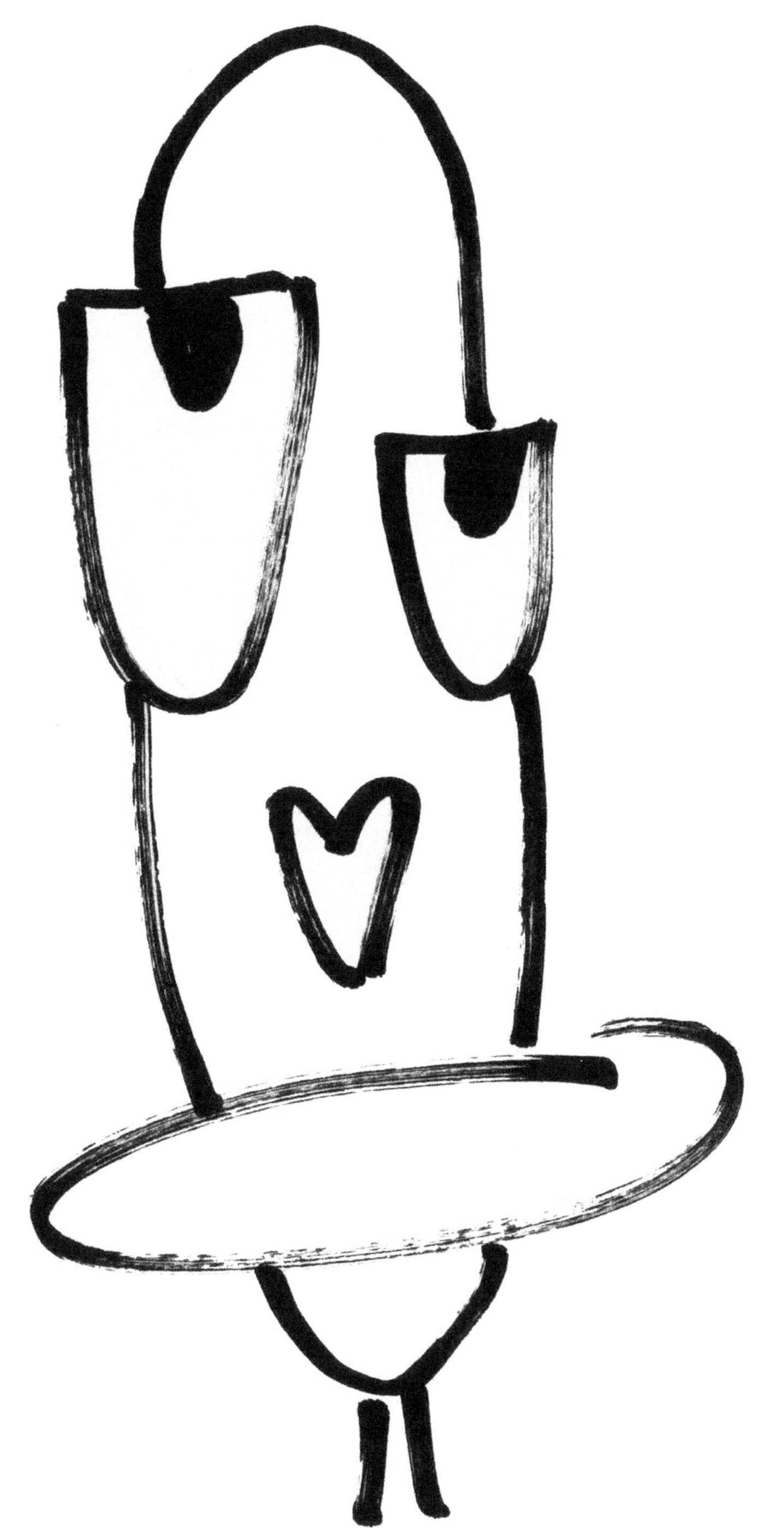

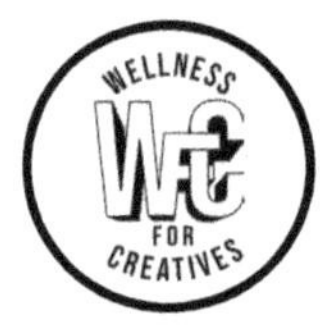

WELL-BEING CHECK-IN

TODAY I FEEL: (CIRCLE ONE)

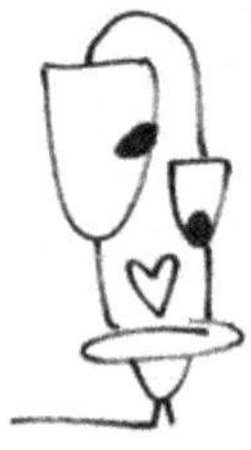 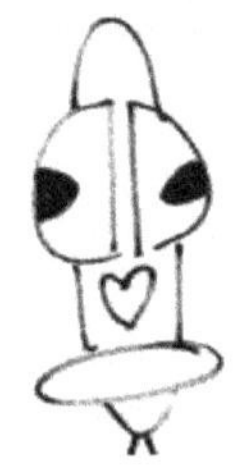 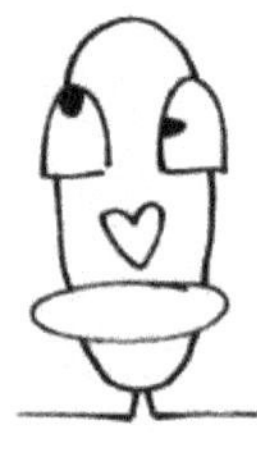 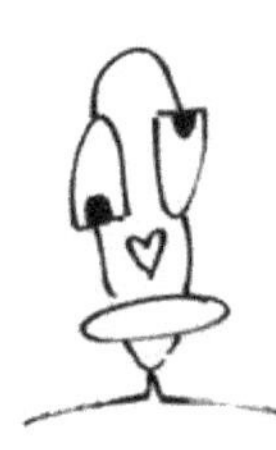 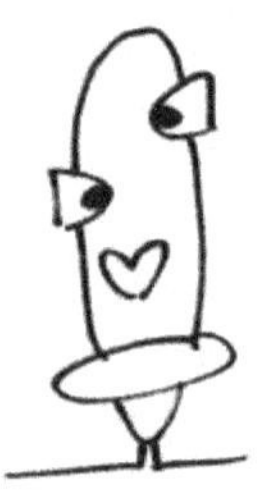

MY MAIN REASON FOR THE ABOVE FEELING IS:

____

____

____

I'M DOING WELL AT:

____

____

____

I NEED HELP WITH:

____

____

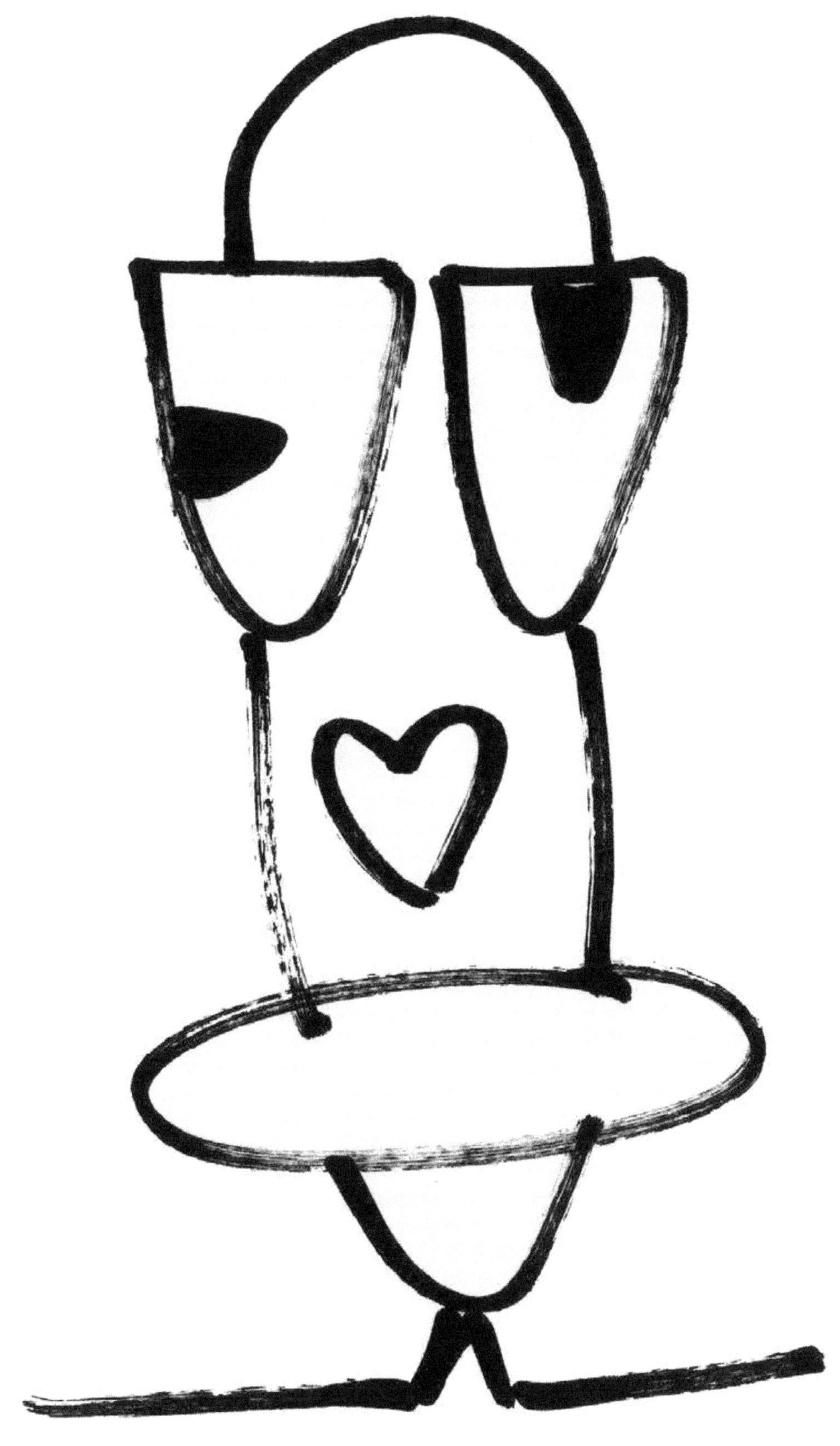

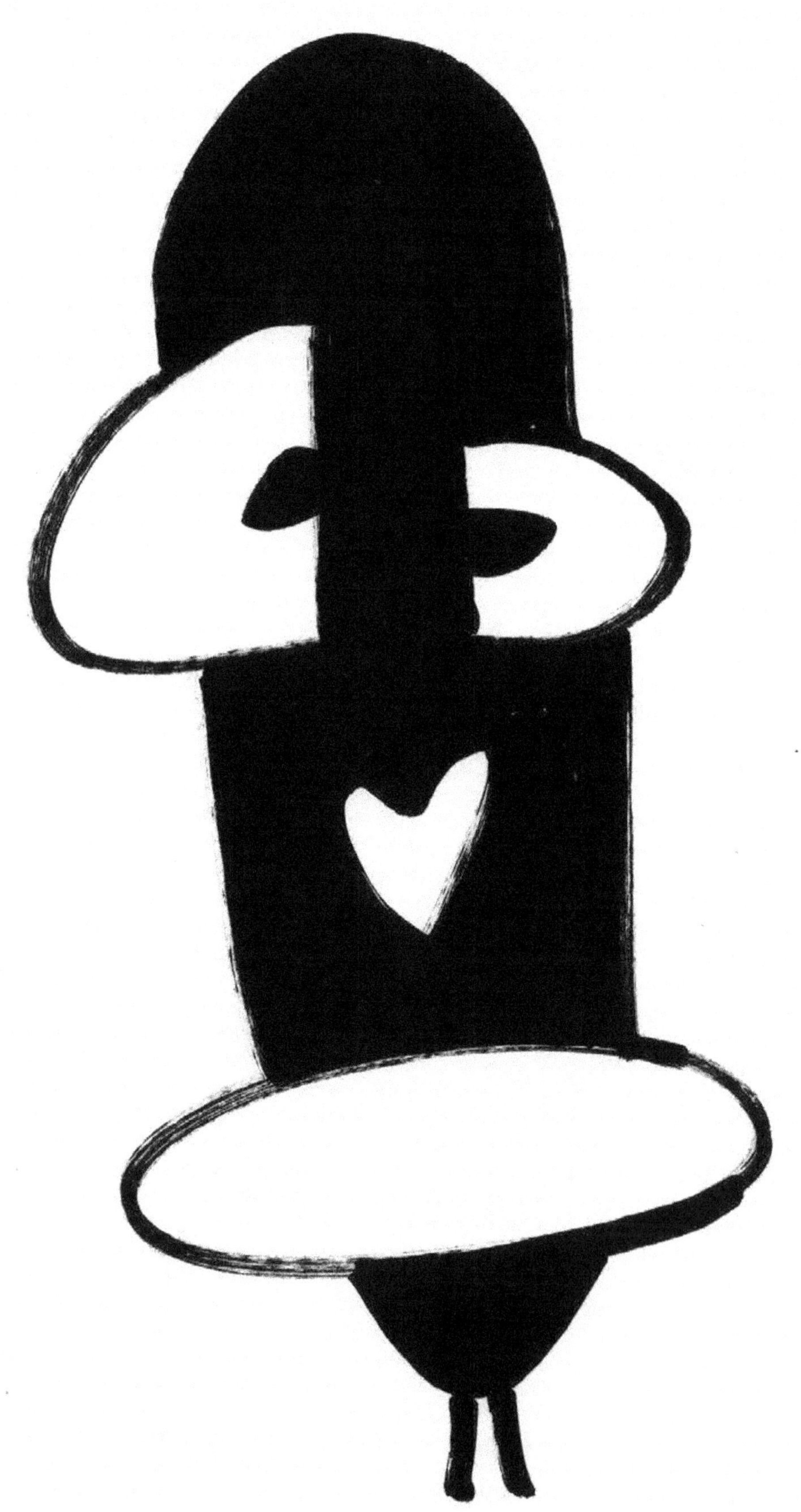

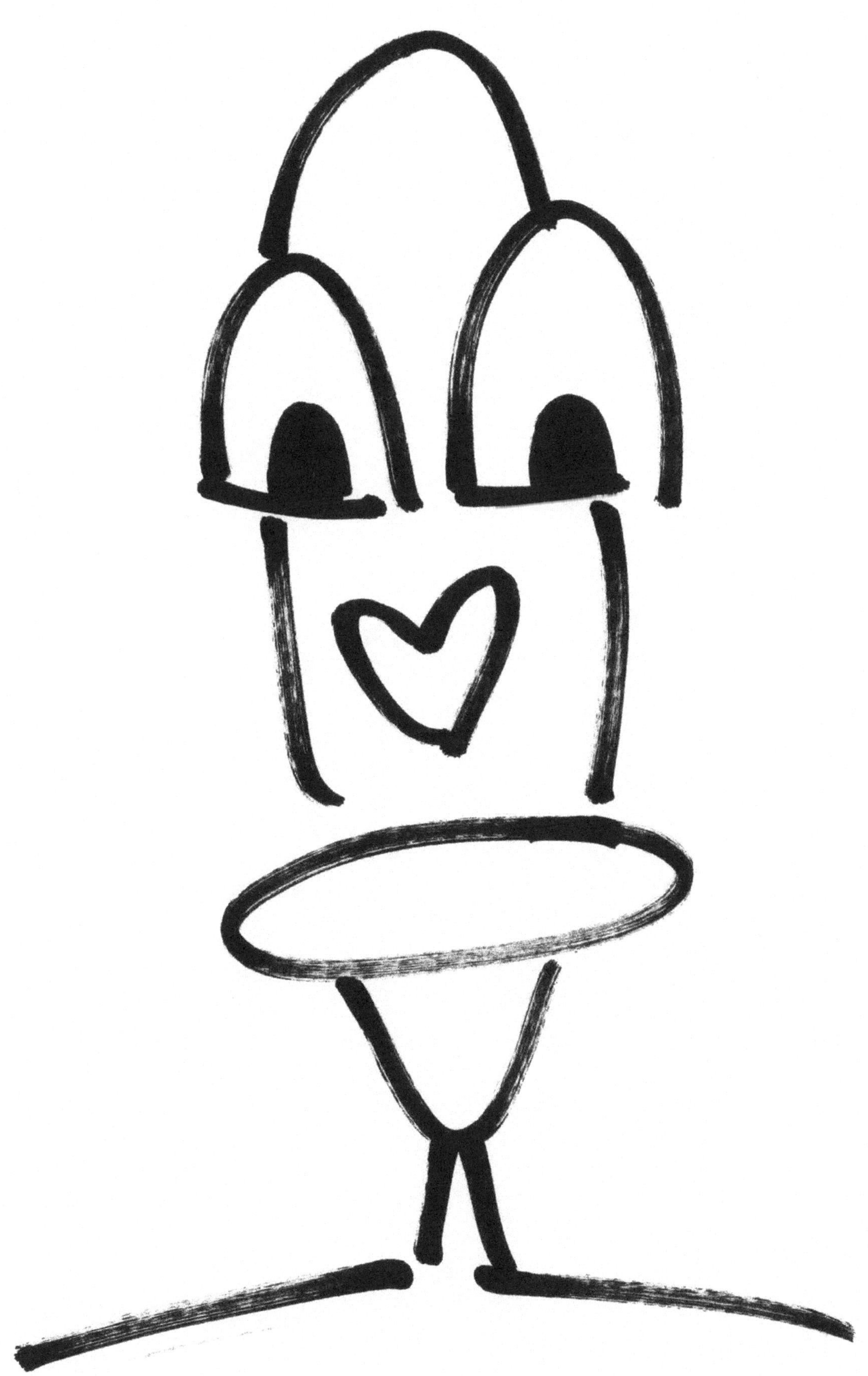

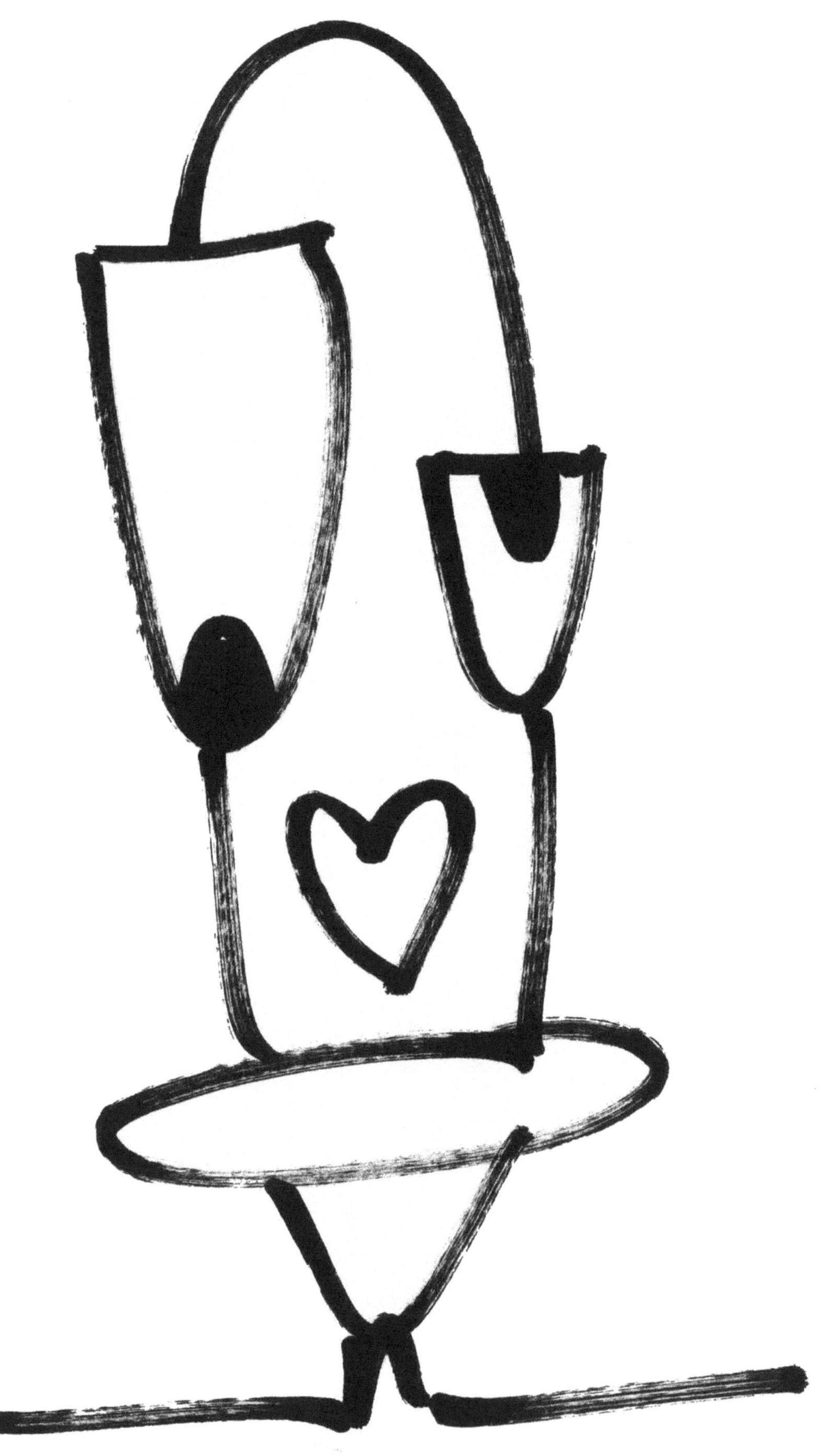

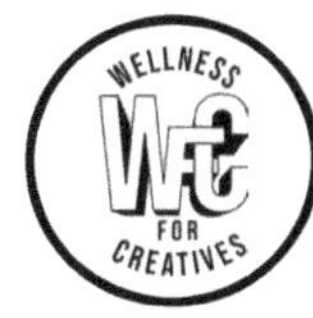

WHAT MAKES ME HAPPY

When I'm happy, ____

____

____

____

____

____

____

____

____

____

____

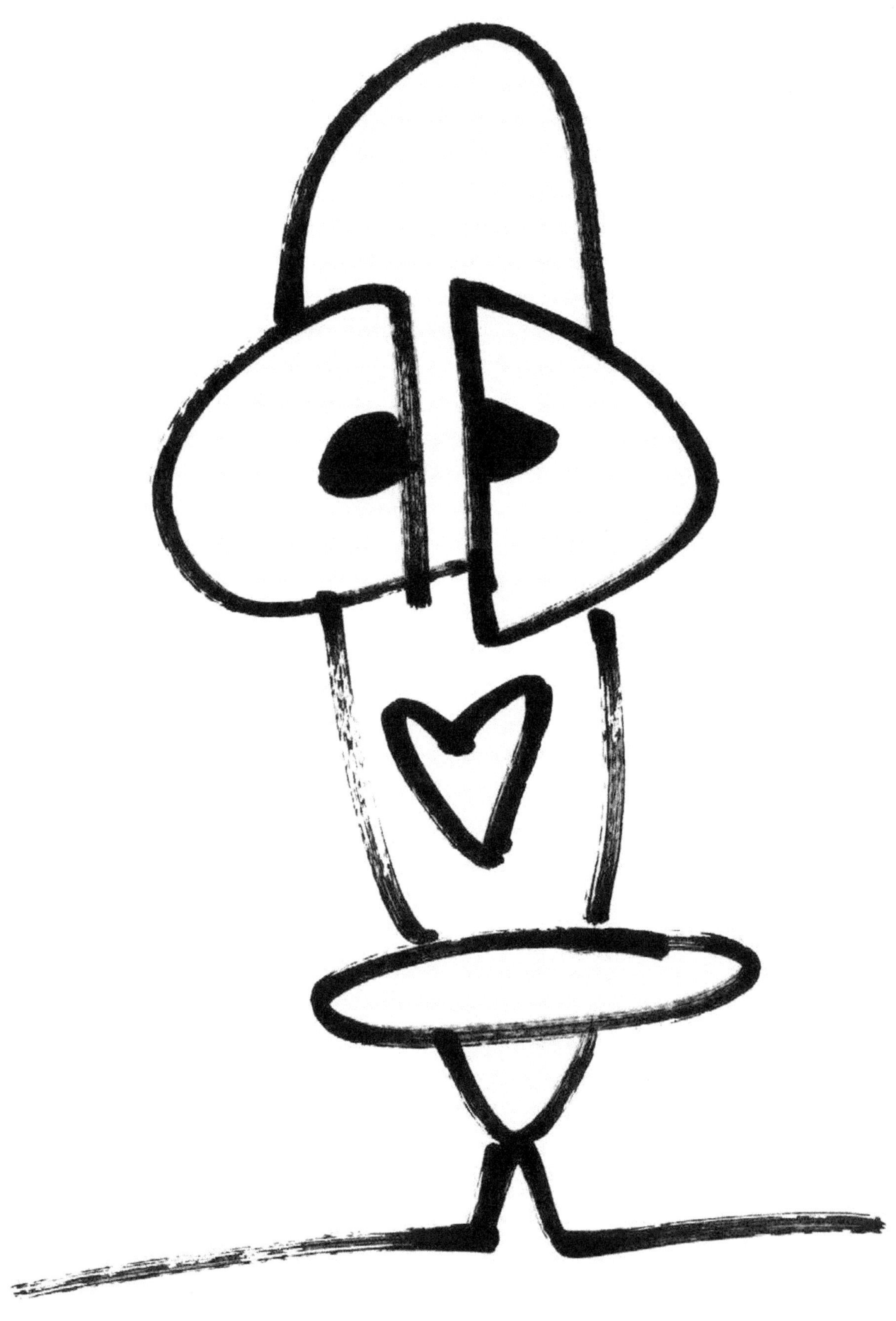

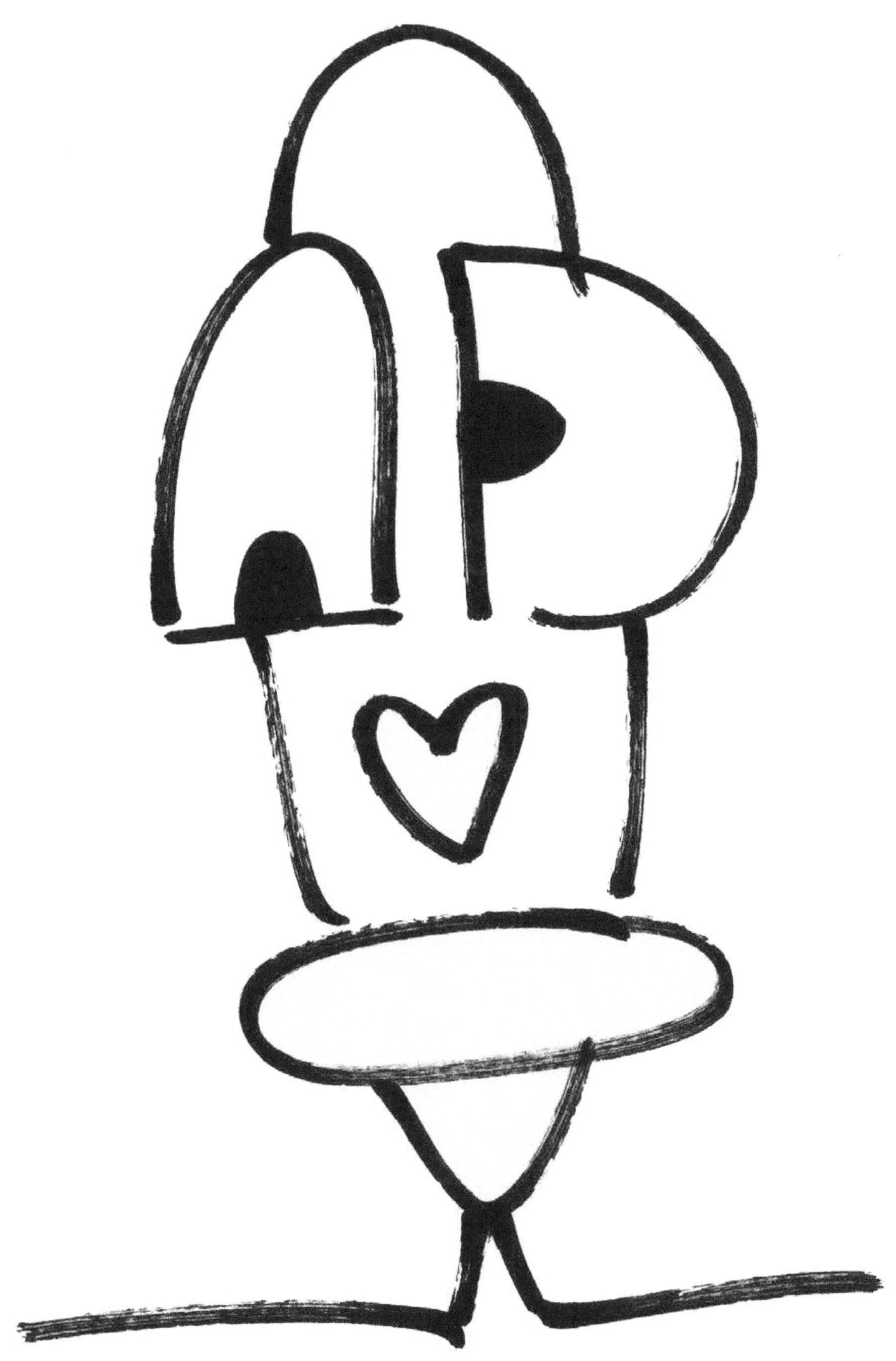

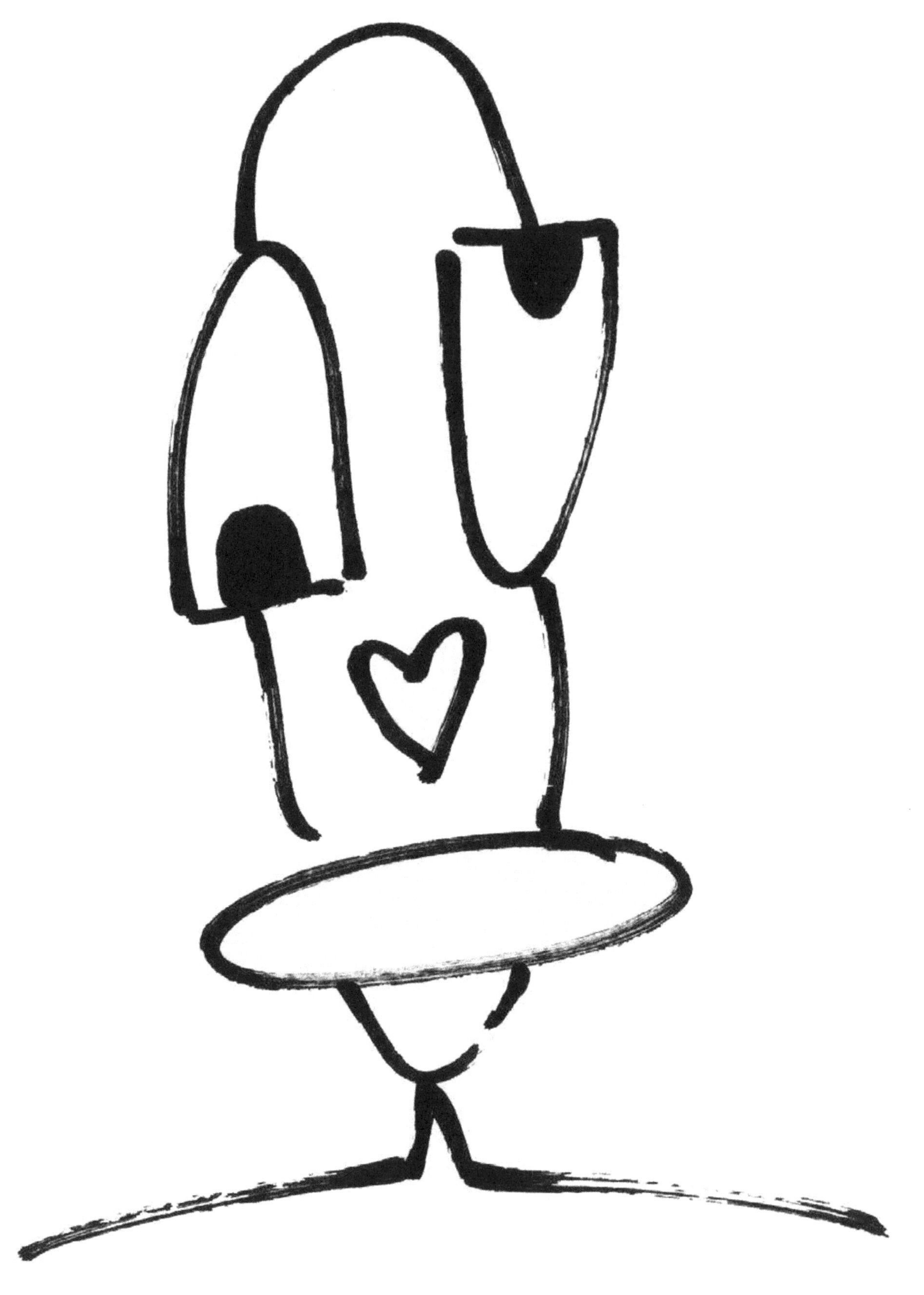

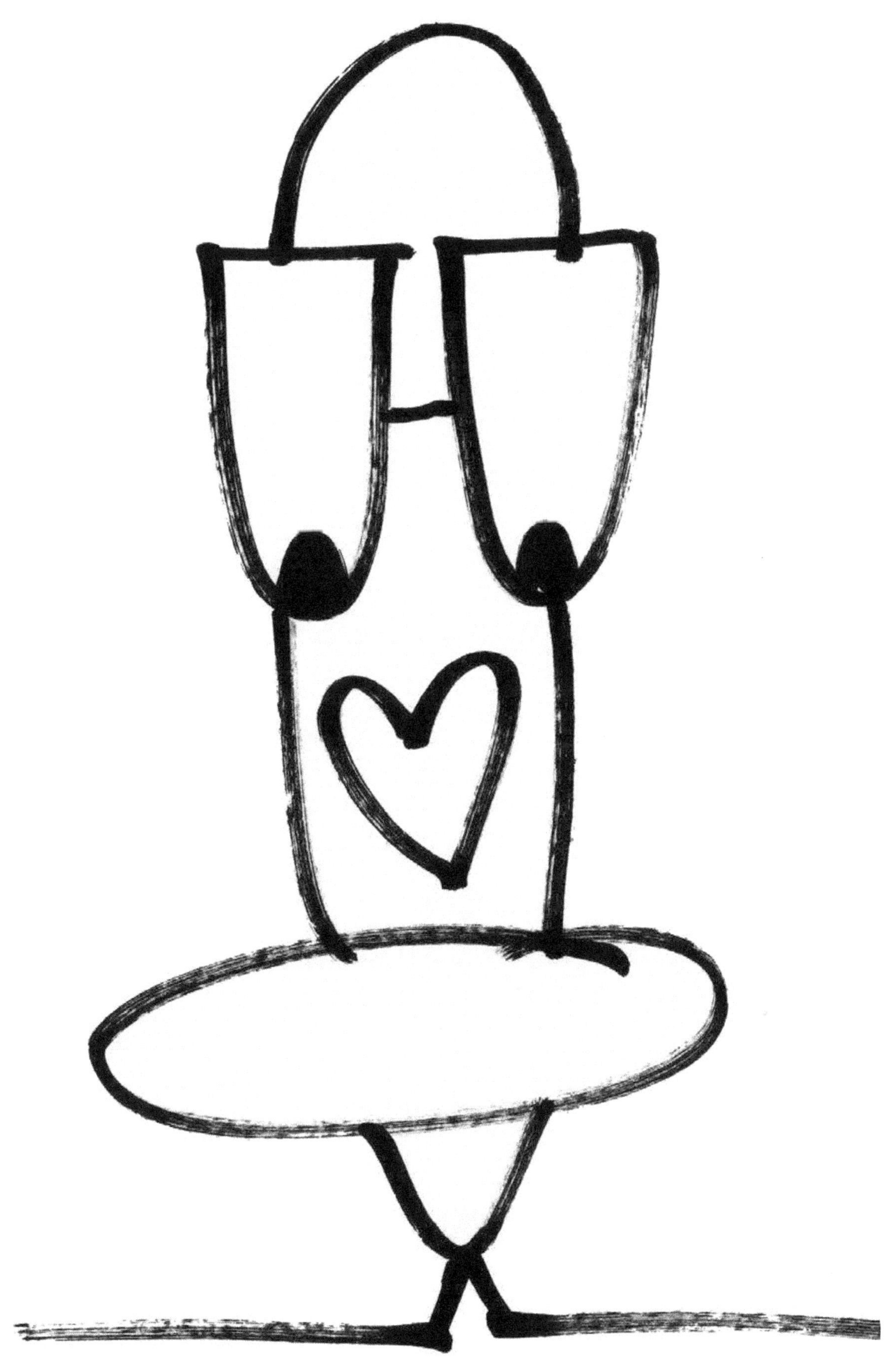

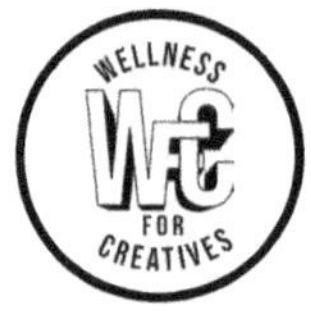

WELL-BEING WEEKLY GOALS

LIVING BY GIVING:

An act of kindness I will complete this week is …

LEARNING AND TRYING:

One goal I am going to try and accomplish this week is …

PURPOSEFUL PRAISE:

One way I will make another person feel appreciated is …

REFLECTING AND ACKNOWLEDGING:

One thing I am proud of achieving this week is…

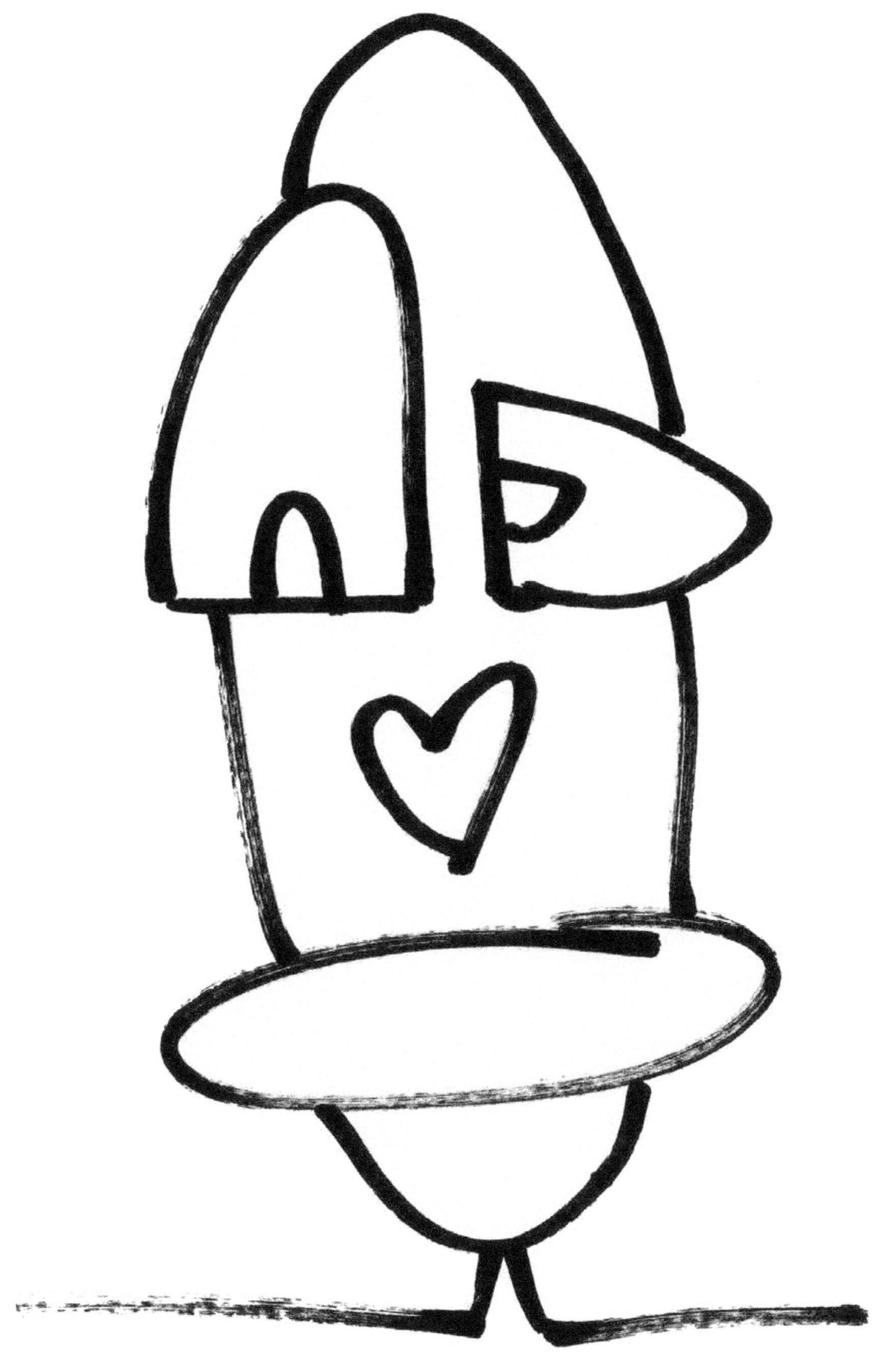

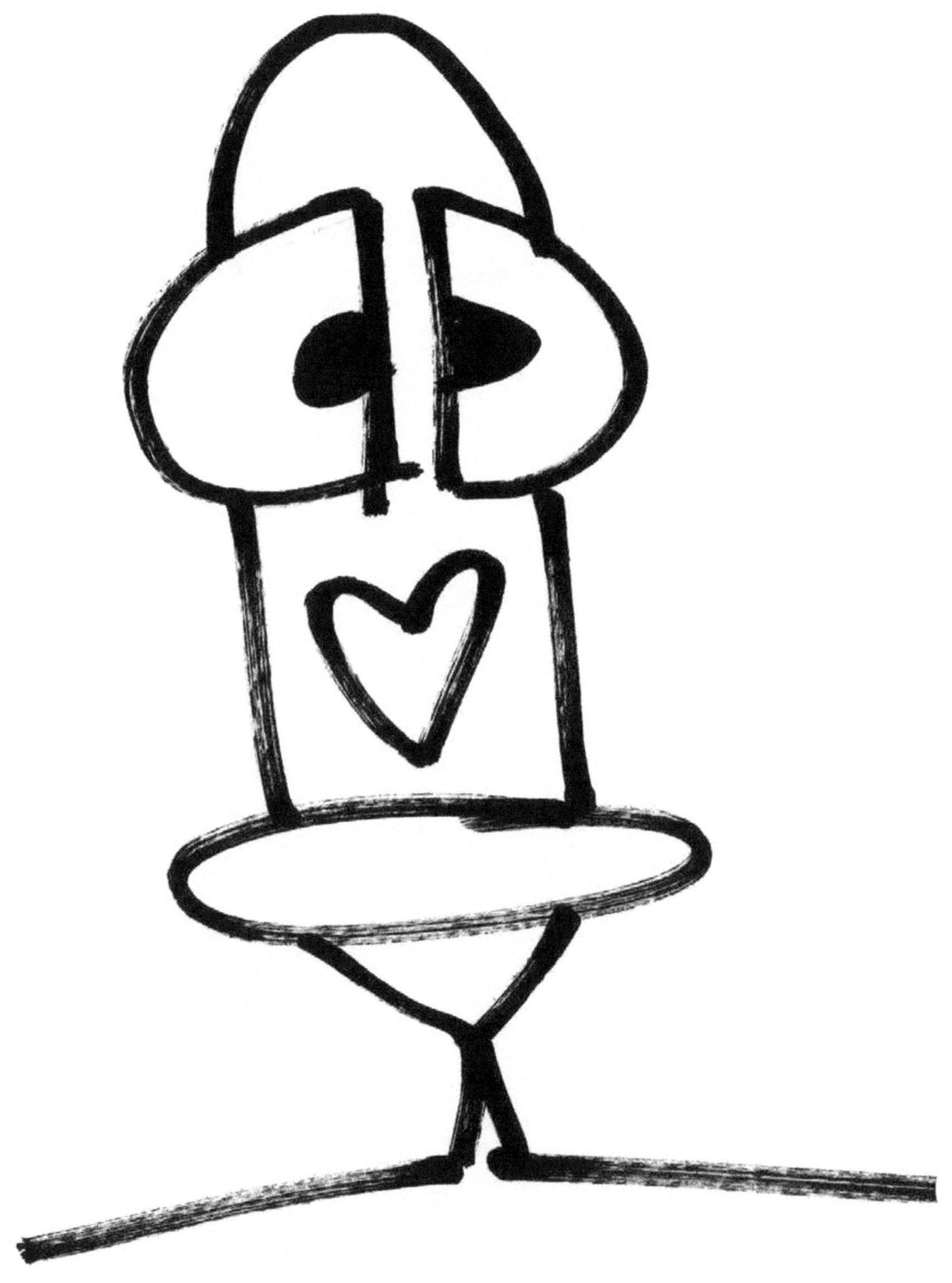

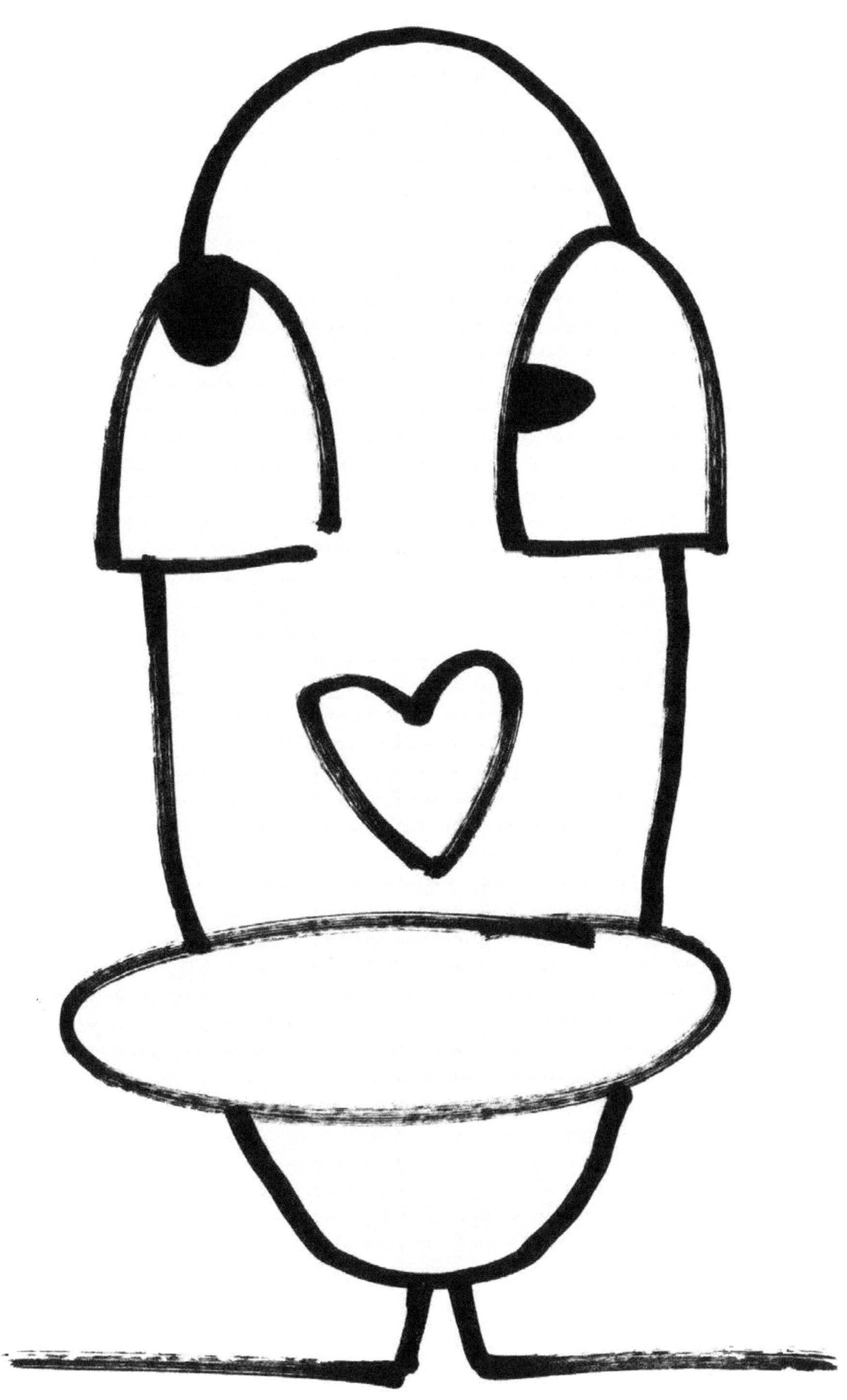

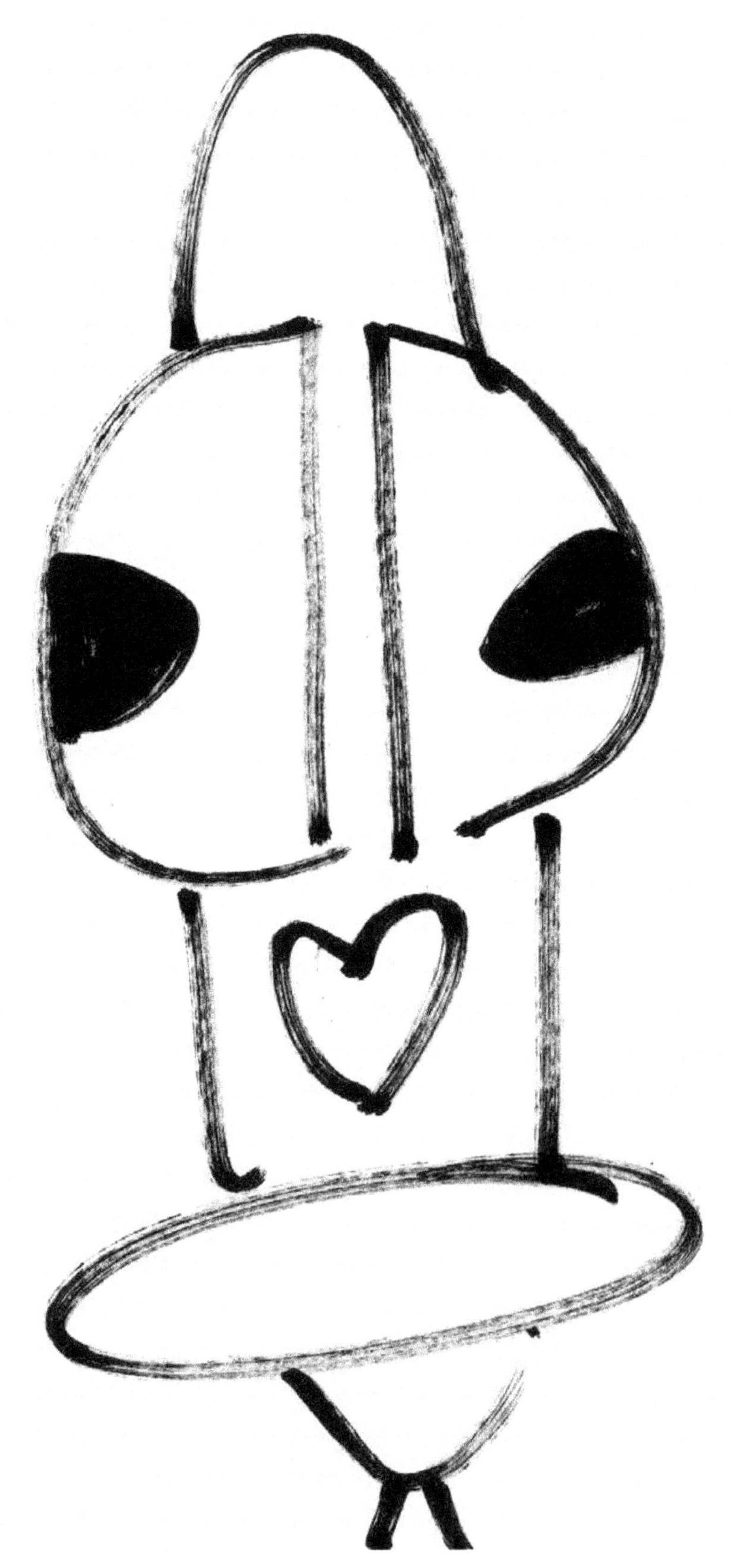

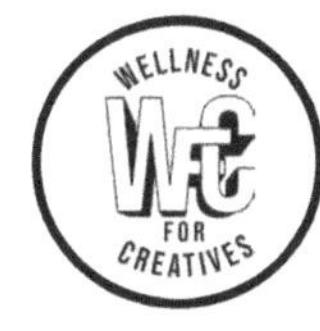

WHAT MAKES ME A "GOOD" PERSON?

Write a paragraph about all the things that make you GOOD.

I'm a good person because...

____

____

____

____

____

____

____

____

____

____

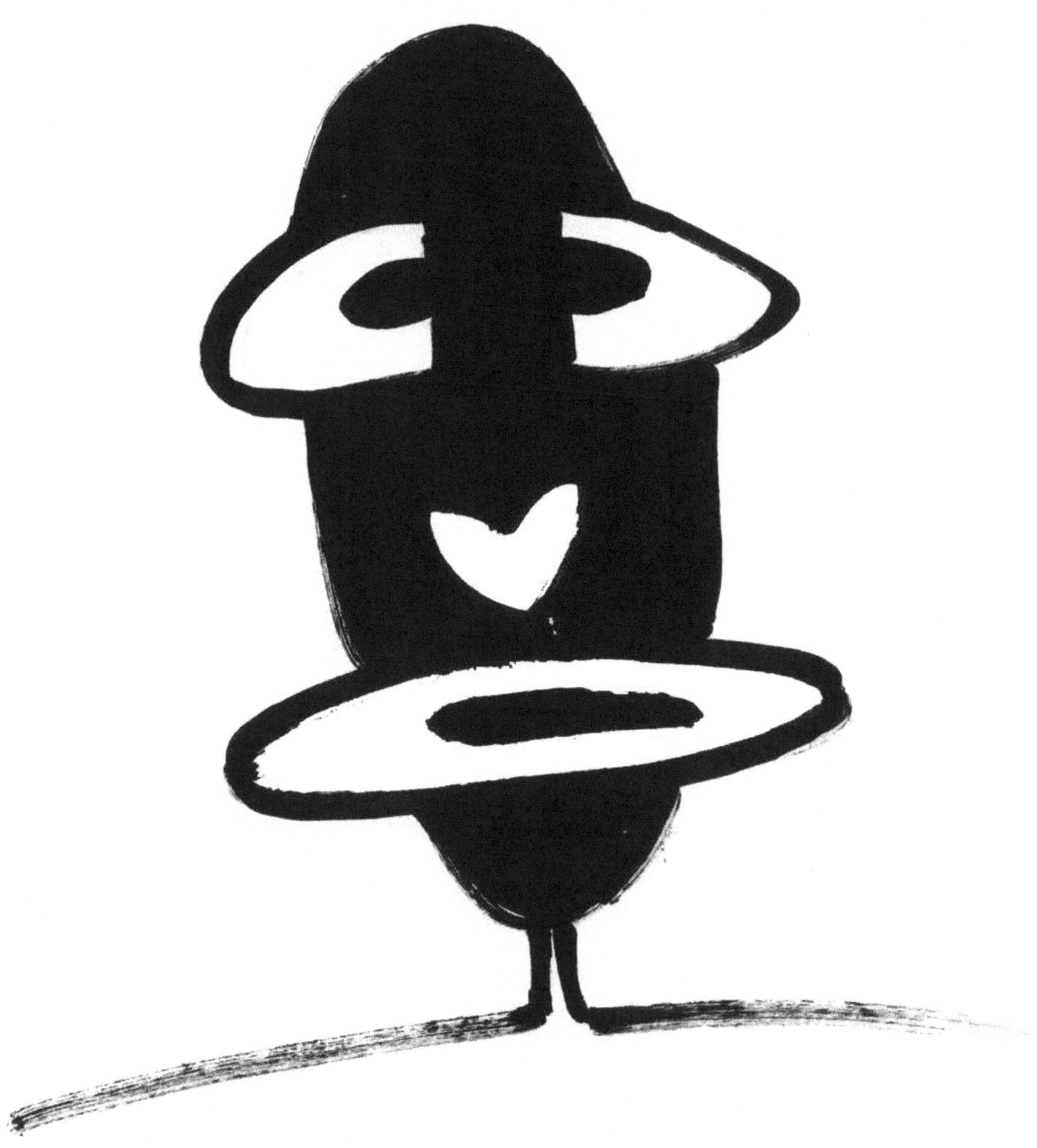

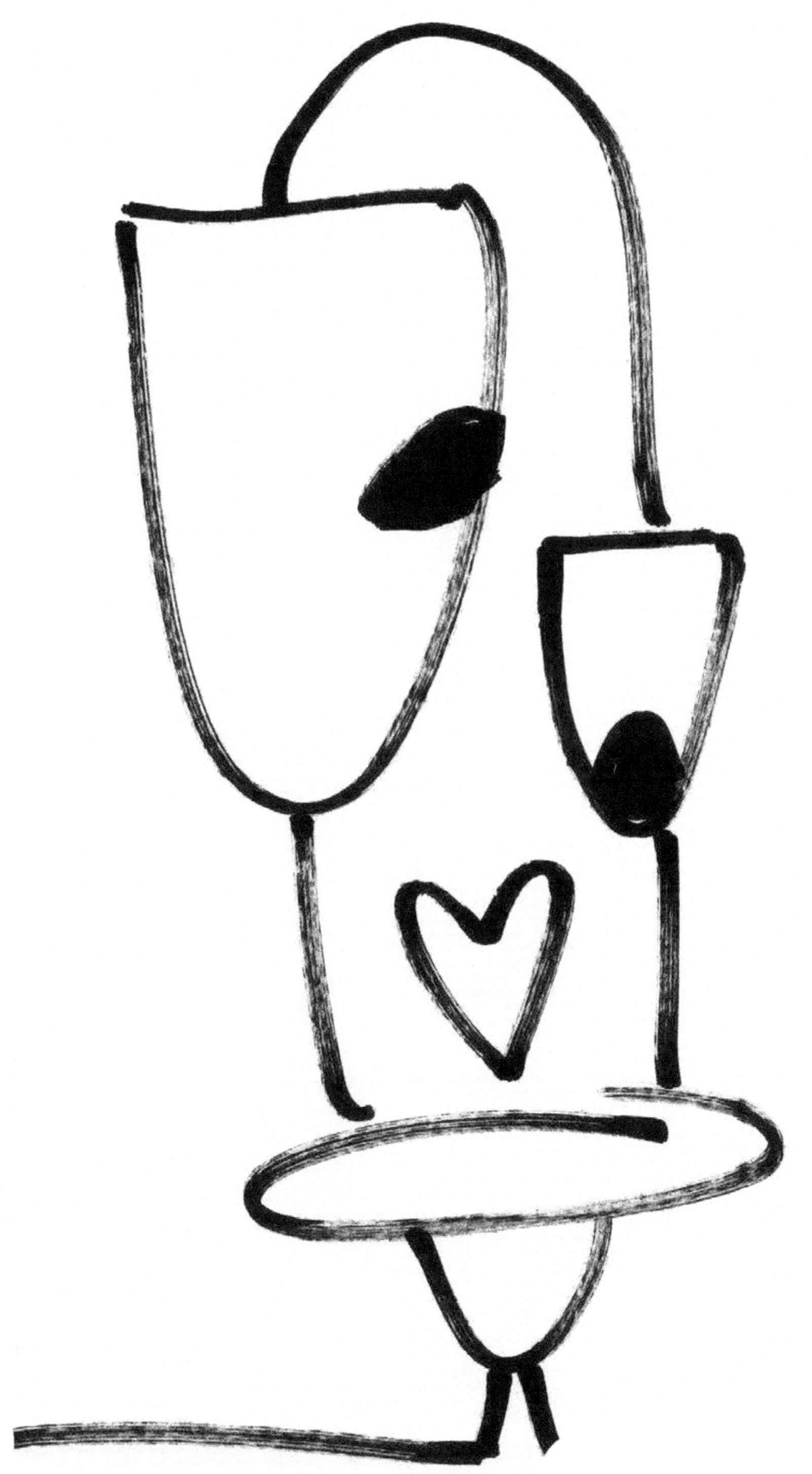

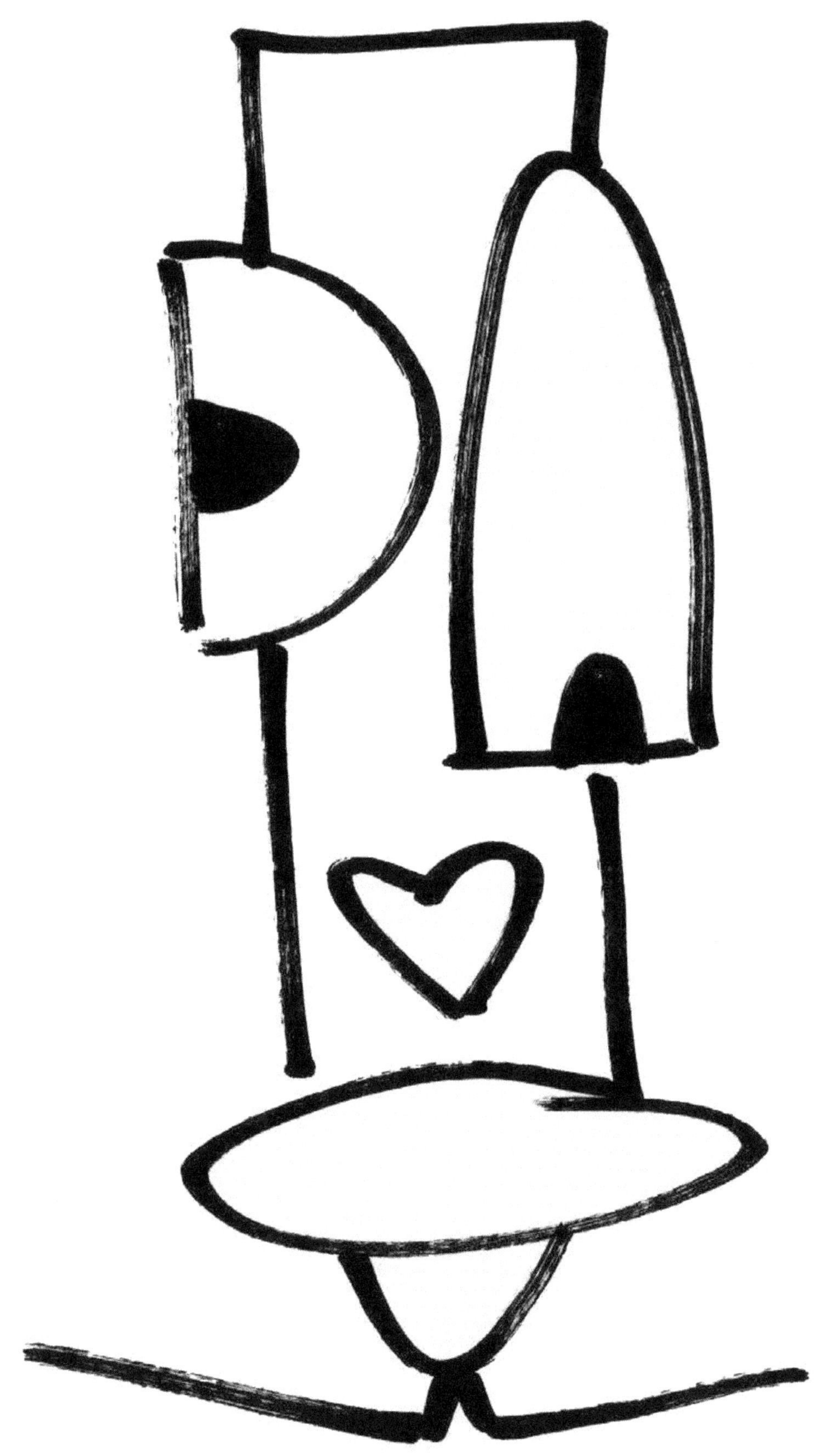

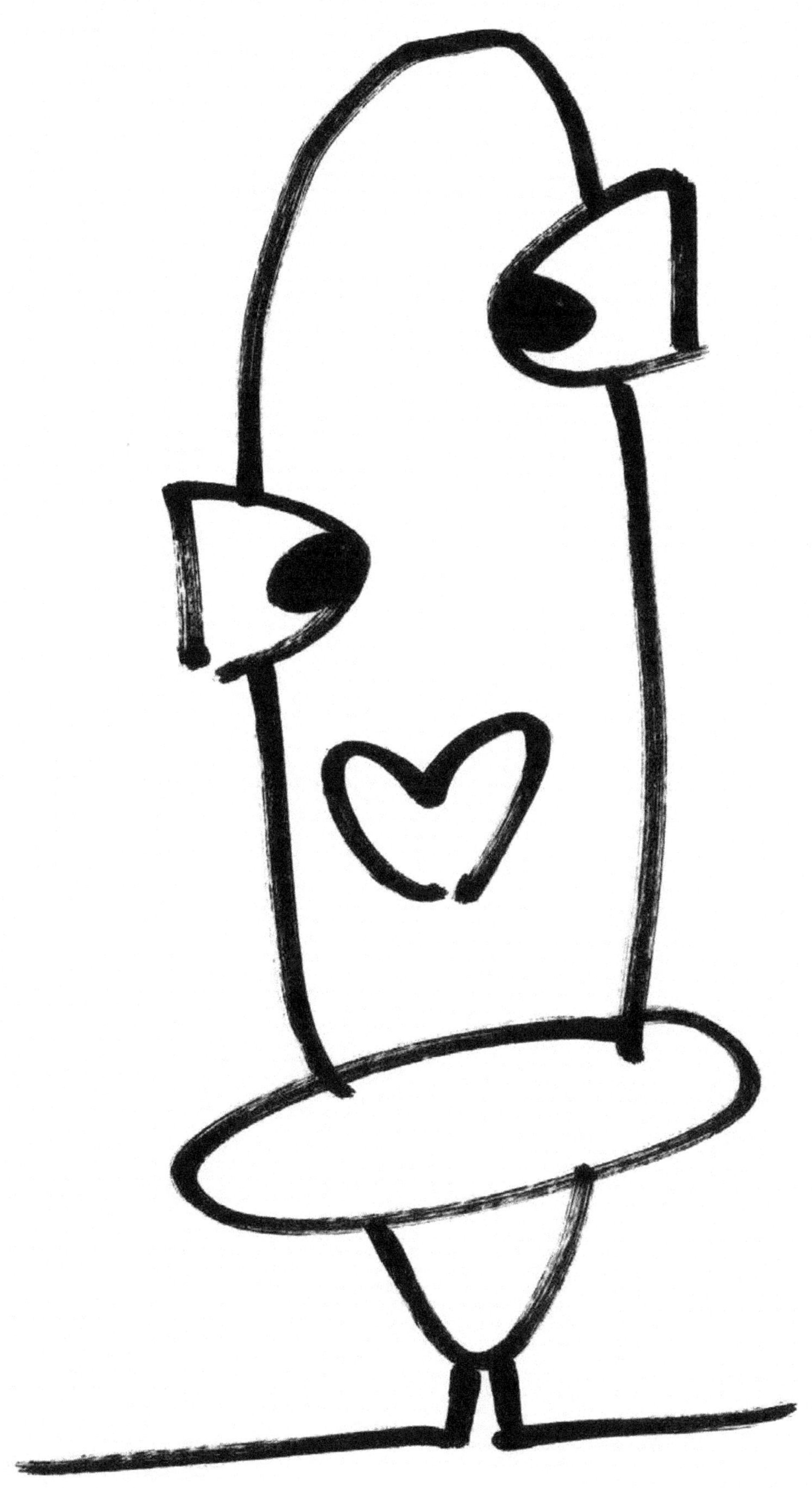

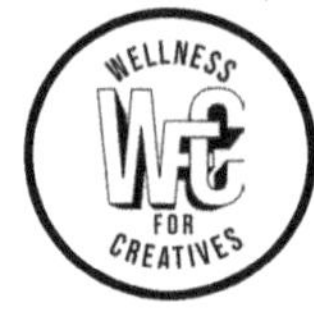

WELL-BEING CHECK-IN

USE THREE WORDS TO DESCRIBE HOW YOU CURRENTLY FEEL:

______________________   ______________________   ______________________

WHY I FEEL THE ABOVE:

HOW PLEASED I AM WITH MY CAREER PROGRESS:

Not at all   Not much   It's okay   Feeling proud

AREA I'D LIKE EXTRA HELP IN:

HOW I FEEL ABOUT MY FRIENDSHIPS / RELATIONSHIPS:

Causing me stress   Having some problems   They're okay   Really well

PEOPLE OR SITUATIONS THAT HAVE MADE ME PROUD THIS WEEK:

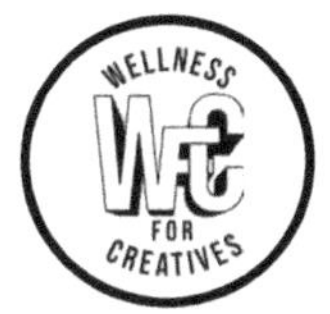

SAFETY NETWORK

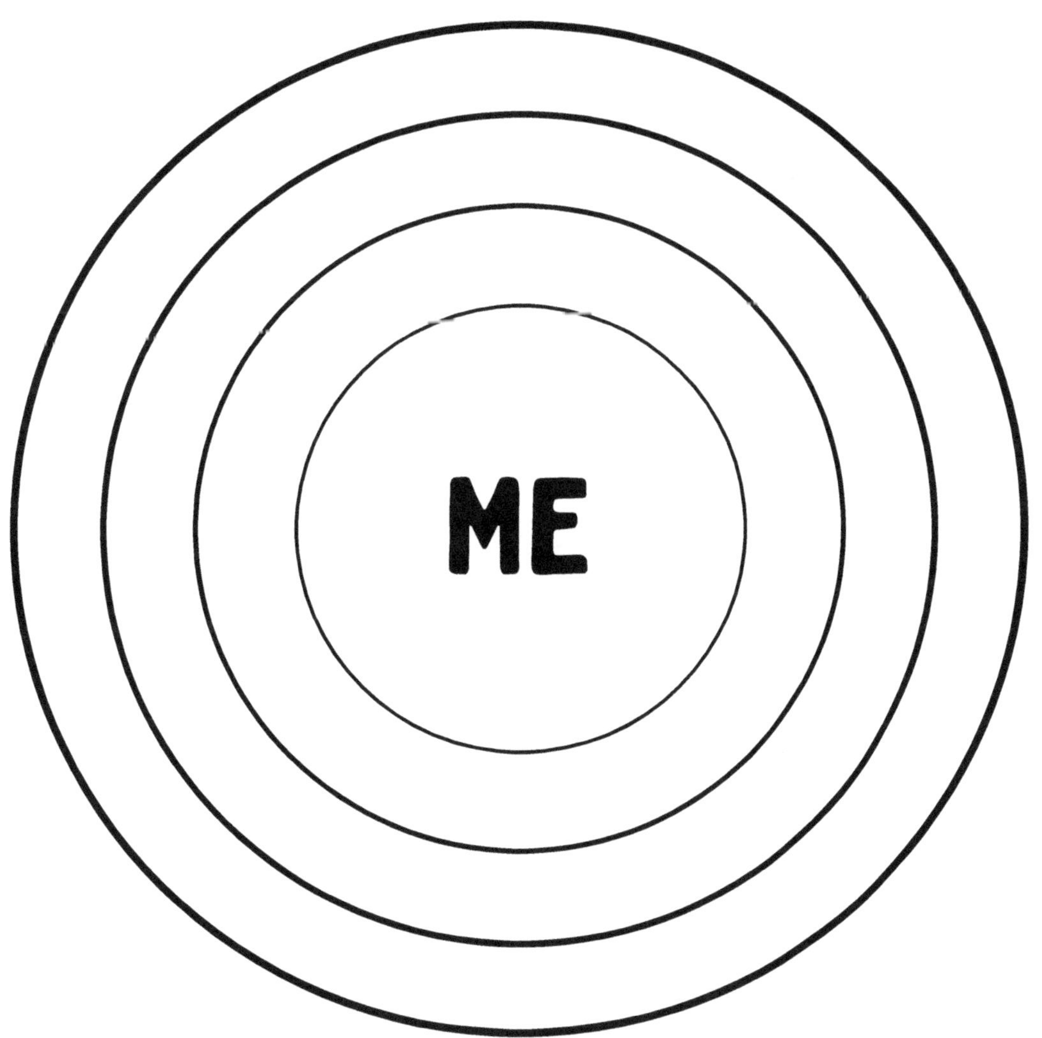

Write the names of your safety network in each layer of the circle. In the circle closest to you, include names of those you trust the most and feel safest with and in the circle farthest from you, include the names of those you trust the least.
For example, the closest circle may be your parents while the farthest may be an employer. Each layer may include more than one name or safety person.

SELF CARE

In the boxes, describe and draw practical ways you can show yourself care